GERARD
MANLEY HOPKINS

The Major Poems

Edited, with an introduction and notes, by

WALFORD DAVIES

Director of Extra-Mural Studies
University College of Wales, Aberystwyth

J. M. Dent & Sons Ltd
London, Melbourne and Toronto
E. P. Dutton & Co. Inc., New York

Phototypeset in V.I.P. Garamond by
Western Printing Services Ltd, Bristol
Printed in Great Britain by
Biddles Ltd, Guildford for
J. M. Dent & Sons Ltd
Aldine House, Welbeck Street, London
First published in Everyman's University Library (U.K.) and
Everyman's Library (U.S.), in 1979

Published in the U.S.A. by arrangement
with J. M. Dent & Sons Ltd

British Library Cataloguing in Publication Data

Hopkins, Gerard Manley
  The major poems.
  I. Davies, Walford
  821'.8   PR4803.H44A17

  ISBN 0–460–10929–4
  ISBN 0–460–11929–X Pbk

Contents

5

Hazel's

Biographical Outline

1844 (28 July)
Born Stratford, Essex: eldest of five brothers, three sisters.

1852
Family moved to Oak Hill, Hampstead.

1854–1863
At Highgate School, near Hampstead: R. W. Dixon (later correspondent) taught there 1861; school gold medal for Latin verse 1862; precocious schoolboy poems in English.

1863 (April)–1867
Classics Exhibitioner, Balliol College, Oxford: initially High Anglican allegiances, like family; start of friendship with Mowbray Baillie and Robert Bridges (later correspondents); received into Roman Catholic Church 21 October 1866; First Class in 'Greats' 1867.
   1863–66: keeps diaries – natural and architectural descriptions and drawings, word-lists, drafts of early poems. 1866 (May)–1875 (Feb.): keeps private Journal – descriptions of minutely observed natural phenomena, images later retrieved in major poems, formulation of 'inscape' and 'instress'; reference 1868 to 'Slaughter of the innocents' i.e. destruction of early poems written 1863–1865.

1867 (Sept.)–1868 (April)
Resident schoolmaster Oratory School, Birmingham, under Cardinal Newman. Decides to become a Jesuit.

1868 (Sept.)–1870 (Sept.)
The 'Novitiate' period as probationer candidate for Jesuit ministry, at Manresa House, Roehampton. Sept. 1870 takes vows of poverty, chastity, obedience.

1870 (Sept.)–1873 (Aug.)
'Philosophate' three-year period of study at St Mary's seminary, Stonyhurst, Lancashire. Summer 1872 first reads Duns Scotus.

1873 (Aug.)–1874 (Aug.)
Teaching at Manresa House, Roehampton.

1874 (Aug.)–1877 (Oct.)
The final 'Theologate' period of training (theological study) at St Beuno's College, Flintshire, N. Wales. December 1875 the wreck of the *Deutschland* leads to resumption of poetic career.

1875 – 'The Wreck of the Deutschland'; 1876 – 'Moonrise', 'The Silver Jubilee', 'Penmaen Pool'; 1877 – 'The Starlight Night', 'God's Grandeur', 'Spring', 'In the Valley of the Elwy', 'The Sea and the Skylark', 'The Windhover', 'Pied Beauty', 'Hurrahing in Harvest', 'The Caged Skylark', 'The Lantern out of Doors'.

Real start of literary correspondence with Robert Bridges April 1877. Final ordination to the Jesuit priesthood September 1877.

1877 (Oct.)–1878 (May)
At Mount St Mary's College, Chesterfield, Derbyshire: administration and temporary teaching.
1878 – 'The Loss of the Eurydice'.

1878 (May–June)
Stonyhurst again, teaching Classics to senior students at the College.
1878 – 'The May Magnificat'.

Correspondence with Canon Dixon begins.

1878 (July–Nov.)
Assistant priest at the Jesuit church of Farm Street, Mayfair.

1878 (Nov.)–1879 (Oct.)
Assistant priest at the new parish church of St Aloysius, Oxford; chaplain to Cowley barracks.
1879 – 'Binsey Poplars', 'Duns Scotus's Oxford', 'Henry Purcell', 'The Candle Indoors', 'The Handsome Heart', 'The Bugler's First Communion', 'Morning Midday and Evening Sacrifice', 'Andromeda', 'Peace'.

1879 (Oct.–Dec.)
Assistant priest at St Joseph's, Bedford Leigh, near Manchester.
1879 – 'At the Wedding March'.

1879 (Dec.)– 1881(Aug.)
Assistant priest at St Francis Xavier's, Liverpool.
1880 – 'Felix Randal', 'Brothers', 'Spring and Fall'.

1881 (Aug.–Oct.)
Temporary parish priest in Glasgow.
1881 – 'Inversnaid', 'As kingfishers catch fire, dragonflies draw flame'.

1881 (Oct.)–1882 (Sept.)
'Tertianship', or 'Second Novitiate' period at Manresa House, Roehampton: study, prayer, and physical work. Final vows in the Society of Jesus taken August 1882.

1882 (Sept.)–1884 (Feb.)
At Stonyhurst again, teaching Classics to senior students at the College.
> *1882 – 'Ribblesdale', 'The Leaden Echo and the Golden Echo' (finished); 1883 – 'The Blessed Virgin compared to the Air we Breathe'.*

Coventry Patmore visits Stonyhurst 1883: start of correspondence.

1884 (Feb.)–1889 (June)
Final period in Dublin as Fellow of the Royal University of Ireland and Professor of Greek at University College, Dublin: lecturing and heavy examining duties. Increasing sense of physical and spiritual collapse articulated especially in so-called 'terrible sonnets' of 1885.
> *1885 – 'Not of all my eyes see, wandering on the world', 'To what serves Mortal Beauty?', 'Spelt from Sibyl's Leaves', terrible sonnets – 'Not, I'll not, carrion comfort, Despair, not feast on thee', 'No worst, there is none', 'I wake and feel the fell of dark, not day', 'Patience, hard thing!', 'My own heart let me more have pity on', 'To seem the stranger lies my lot, my life'; 'Yes. Why do we all, seeing of a soldier, bless him?'; 1887 – 'Tom's Garland', 'Harry Ploughman'; 1888 – 'That Nature is a Heraclitean Fire and of the comfort of the Resurrection', 'In honour of St Alphonsus Rodriguez'; 1889 – 'Thou art indeed just, Lord, if I contend with thee', 'The shepherd's brow, fronting forked lightning', 'To R. B.'*

Hopkins dies of typhoid fever 8 June 1889, aged forty-five.

Select Bibliography

I THE TEXTS

The Poems of G. M. Hopkins, 4th edn., edited by W. H. Gardner and N. H. MacKenzie, London, 1967

The Journals and Papers of G. M. Hopkins, edited by H. House and G. Storey, London, 1959

The Sermons and Devotional Writings of G. M. Hopkins, edited by C. Devlin S. J., London, 1959

Letters of G. M. Hopkins to Robert Bridges, revised edn., edited by C. C. Abbott, London, 1955

Correspondence of G. M. Hopkins and R. W. Dixon, revised edn., edited by C. C. Abbott, London, 1956

Further Letters of G. M. Hopkins, revised edn., edited by C. C. Abbott, London, 1956

2 BIOGRAPHICAL

A. Thomas S. J., *Hopkins the Jesuit: the Years of Training*, London, 1969

B. Bergonzi, *Gerard Manley Hopkins*, London, 1977

P. Kitchen, *Gerard Manley Hopkins*, London, 1978

3 CRITICAL

W. H. Gardner, *Gerard Manley Hopkins*, 2 vols., London, 1944, 1949

G. Grigson, *Gerard Manley Hopkins* ('Writers and their Work' series), London, 1955

G. H. Hartman ed., *Hopkins: A Collection of Critical Essays* ('Twentieth Century Views' series), Englewood Cliffs, N. J., 1966

N. H. MacKenzie, *Hopkins* ('Writers and Critics' series), Edinburgh, 1968

E. W. Schneider, *The Dragon in the Gate*, Berkeley and Los Angeles, 1968

M. Bottrall ed., *Gerard Manley Hopkins: Poems* ('Casebook' series), London, 1975

J. Milroy, *The Language of Gerard Manley Hopkins*, London, 1978

F. R. Leavis, 'Gerard Manley Hopkins' in *New Bearings in English Poetry*, London, 1932

D. Davie, 'Hopkins as a Decadent Critic' in *Purity of Diction in English Verse*, London, 1952

B. Hardy, *Forms and Feelings in the Sonnets of Gerard Manley Hopkins*, 1st Annual Lecture of the Hopkins Society, London, 1970

A. Llwyd, '*Cynghanedd* and English Poetry', *Poetry Wales* XIV, 1, Swansea, 1978

4 COMMENTARY

P. L. Mariani, *A Commentary on the Complete Poems of Gerard Manley Hopkins*, Cornell, 1969

5 BIBLIOGRAPHY

T. Dunne, *Gerard Manley Hopkins: A Comprehensive Bibliography*, London, 1976

Note on Selection and Text

This edition is of all the complete poems written during Hopkins's major period, 1875–89. They are the works on which his reputation as a major poet rests. To these have been added two other poems from within the period, but which Hopkins considered revising: 'Moonrise' and the poem beginning 'Not of all my eyes see, wandering on the world'. The revisions contemplated were slight, and the two poems are included not only for their impressive quality but because their first versions, as printed here, seem to the editor also to be the best ones.

The text used is that of Robert Bridges's first edition of 1918. Ten minor points of spelling, punctuation, or line-indentation (five of which were emended in the second edition of 1930) are silently corrected here. Another six points have been corrected as follows: the full-stop instead of a comma in lines 37 and 85 of 'The Loss of the Eurydice'; the exclamation-mark instead of a question-mark in line 13 of 'The Handsome Heart'; *O is he dead then?* instead of *O he is dead then?* in line 1 of 'Felix Randal'; the original *reeve* instead of Bridges's substituted *handle* in line 10 of 'Yes. Why do we all, seeing of a soldier, bless him?'; and the original *combs* instead of Bridges's substituted *moulds* in line 6 of 'To R. B.' Three poems for which Bridges provided titles are returned to their untitled form.

Introduction

I

> The nearer hills, the other side of the valley, shewed a hard and
> beautifully detached and glimmering brim against the light,
> which was lifting there. All the length of the valley the skyline of
> hills was flowingly written all along upon the sky. A blue bloom, a
> sort of meal, seemed to have spread upon the distant south,
> enclosed by a basin of hills. Looking all around but most in looking
> far up the valley I felt an instress and charm of Wales.[1]

Thus a private journal entry of 6 September 1874. Its author,
Gerard Manley Hopkins, at the age of thirty, had newly arrived
at St Beuno's College in Flintshire, North Wales. There, during
the next three years, he completed the final period of training
leading to his ordination as a Jesuit priest. It was at this place
and time that many things came fully home to him.

The previous ten years had already been a period of momentous decisions, radiating from his conversion to Roman Catholicism as a classics undergraduate ('the star of Balliol') at Oxford
in 1866. It had been a period when, especially in the atmosphere
of debate and inquiry at the university, questions of Anglican
belief and loyalties were subject to the pressure of two broad
opposite forces. On the one hand there was the general liberalizing tendency of the age which, on the other, intensified the
questions of tradition and authority. In a climate of increasing
Rationalist secularization, the Broad Church position minim-
ized dogma and strove to reconcile developments in modern
thought with Christianity, while the Low or Evangelical
Church counteracted by placing its faith in the strict authority
of scripture. Neither questioned the historical authenticity of
the Church of England itself. Within that church, there had
still remained another conservative possibility for any devout
young man making a decision at that time. This was the High
Church or 'Tractarian' position, which had been headed at
Oxford by leaders like Pusey and Liddon, and to which Hopkins

13

had naturally given his first allegiance. Ever since the Oxford Movement of the 1830s, when *Tracts for the Times* had been published, this body of thought had articulated and strengthened the Anglo-Catholic stand against the levelling tendencies within the church. It insisted that the Church of England was itself Catholic, and that its bishops represented a true Apostolic succession. It also satisfied the ritualistic tendency of the young Hopkins. But it did not accept the Roman Catholic principle of papal supremacy. This had been the stumbling block for Hopkins (as two decades earlier it had been for John Henry Newman, whose account of his own conversion to Roman Catholicism in his *Apologia Pro Vita Sua* had been published during Hopkins's second year at Oxford); it had prevented his continuing in a church which otherwise he already, both aesthetically and dogmatically, accepted.

The conversion had meant a traumatic break from the moderate High Anglican traditions of his family, and his parents' expectations for their eldest child. It was a filial break which was to remain as intellectually painful at the end of his short life (when, in Ireland, he wrote the sonnet 'To seem the stranger lies my lot, my life') as it had been initially bitter, when Hopkins's father had actively sought to prevent the conversion. This filial trauma was gradually compounded by its also being a break with the order of things in England. Hopkins's profound Victorian-patriotic love for his country ('wife/To my creating thought')[2] intensified as an even deeper love-in-estrangement. His decision, in 1868, to go further along the road and become a Jesuit priest had placed the separation beyond questions of mere private beliefs. Now, as a follower of St Ignatius Loyola, founder of the Counter-Reformation order of the Jesuits, Hopkins was dedicating himself to a disciplined intellectual *exploration* of those beliefs, and to the responsibility of militantly directing them towards the reconversion of Britain to Roman Catholicism. Though to a realist this might appear only a notional Jesuit aim, its totality of vision alone could measure the zeal and relentless self-sacrifice which was to mark Hopkins's career throughout. Certainly, a refusal to accept the notional, the tendency to act, both privately and publicly, as if out of a state of emergency, characterized everything he was to do.

Equipped intellectually to have been the ablest Catholic apologist of his age, his fate after the St Beuno period, however, was to serve in practical-pastoral and teaching duties for which he was physically and temperamentally less well equipped. These duties were also to mean that most of his philosophical-scholarly projects, entertained or started, had to be abandoned. His Jesuit service was to take the form of teaching at various of the order's colleges, and periods as assistant priest at churches in London, Oxford, Manchester, Liverpool and Glasgow. Experience of the sordid industrial conditions in places like Liverpool and Glasgow was to appall the sensibility of one who took nature as a norm and not a luxury. Finally, in 1884, he was to be appointed Fellow of the Royal University of Ireland and Professor of Greek at University College, Dublin. His lectures, like his sermons throughout, showed an unsure grasp of the needs of an individual, particular audience, being executed often at too meticulous and demanding a level. This was, however, the same kind of demand that he was to make on his own physical and nervous resources throughout his life, interpreting the role of private discipline well beyond the actual demands of his order, and being often his own worst enemy on the question of his personal spiritual deservingness. But the hard reality of demands outside himself was not always simply imagined. A frail though wiry constitution meant that the colossal burden of lecturing and examination-marking during his last five years in Dublin ('it is killing work to examine a nation') was to bring ever nearer the reality of physical as well as spiritual collapse. He was to die of typhoid, at the age of forty-five, in 1889.

But we are interested in the man who wrote as he did in his journal in 1874, not simply because of his beliefs and decisions as a man, or the fate of that outward career. He was also a poet. That, above all else, is what that journal entry shows. In any case, his deepest biography is only available in the 'rehearsal of own, of abrupt self'[3] that his particular kind of poetry was ultimately to make possible. It is in many ways a poetry more accessible to the post-Modernist poetic expectations of our own time than it could ever have been to those of his own day, despite the necessary exclusiveness of his theological beliefs and the essentially Victorian nature of much in his interests and sensibility. Robert Bridges (the Oxford friend who, along with one or two other correspondents, constituted his only poetic audience during his lifetime) judged happily in delaying the main publication of the poems until 1918, twenty-nine years after the poet's death.

At St Beuno's in 1874, however, Hopkins had already made another momentous and characteristically quiet decision – to sacrifice the poetry. The metaphoric journal entry which in 1868 had signalled the destruction of his undergraduate poems – the 'Slaughter of the innocents'[4] – itself reflects the agony this had involved. Earlier references had attested the same regret: 'On this day by God's grace I resolved to give up all beauty until I had His leave for it'.[5] And later remarks still echoed this telling hope that one day the poet and the priest could be officially, and *jointly*, sanctioned: he told R. W. Dixon in 1878 that he had resolved 'to write no more, as not belonging to my profession, unless it were by the wish of my superiors'.[6] That sanction came in the wake of a tragic event of 7 December 1875. The *Deutschland*, a ship bound from Bremen to New York, via Southampton, was wrecked in the mouth of the Thames. Among the drowned were five Franciscan nuns, refugees from the anti-clerical Falk Laws in Germany. The fact that there were no attempts at early rescue, although the ship took over twenty-four hours to sink, made the event a national scandal, reported in tragic detail in *The Times* and the *Illustrated London News*. But it was the death of the nuns that focused Hopkins's interpretation of the tragedy when, in response to his Rector's spontaneous wish that someone should commemorate the event in a poem, Hopkins wrote 'The Wreck of the Deutschland'.

Having since 1868 written only 'two or three little presentation pieces',[7] he felt that the opportunity to embark on the first of his major poems had come unsought. In that sense, it brought effective freedom from any feeling that his poetry was a private luxury, at odds with the chosen rigours of his training and ultimate calling. It is likely that that tension between artistic impulse and impersonal duty was something Hopkins modestly suspected, and obediently respected, rather than felt on his pulses, as it were. Poetry, painting and music had been areas of natural interest and real talent manifested early in his upbringing, and by other members of his family. The location of St Beuno's also reaffirmed another deep-set fact: it was the same quality – an unusually alert responsiveness to living nature – that fed his poetic impulse as confirmed his theology. The world of nature he always felt to be truth-revealing, and its celebration consonant with any Christian duty to reveal and obey God. Poetry arising from such an impulse would be a luxury only if it failed to gain direction in the creative service of faith. Equally important, it would be an indulgence only if new ways of seeing nature and of harnessing language failed to make that poetic impulse fresh, authentic, and inevitable.

The point is that the St Beuno's period dovetailed many intellectual discoveries that the poet had made during his seven years of virtual poetic silence. Given the force of those discoveries, ascetic feelings of guilt at being a poet were to prove less of a danger than the sense of frustration at having to be a secret one. Although he modestly accepted his obscurity, he was also to become firmly convinced that a certain measure of respect and esteem was necessary to the creative process. The late sonnet 'Thou art indeed just, Lord, if I contend with thee' springs, not from guilt at being a poet, but from the trauma of feeling the spontaneous sources of that poetry failing. To some degree the healthy need for a response to his work was also given sublimated expression in the sense of religious alienation in those later poems: 'cries like dead letters sent/To dearest him that lives alas! away'.[8] Isolation from the ever-increasing audience for literature in Victorian England worked to his advantage in enabling him to develop what was most eccentric and revolutionary in his idiom without the need to compromise and without the ridicule that failing to compromise would entail. But even his restricted audience did not always smooth the path of that obscurity. The refusal of the Jesuit journal *The Month* to publish 'The Wreck of the Deutschland' in 1875 proved a forecast of the critical blankness felt by Hopkins's correspondents, even Bridges in certain ways, in the face of the poetry's technical adventurousness. It could not, however, end the impulse to create. That impulse was given a new and rich sustenance at St Beuno's, quite apart from the Jesuitical 'opportunity' of the *Deutschland*'s tragedy. The individuating powers of language Hopkins saw as complementary, and complimentary, to the endlessly unique beauties of the created world itself. In this, one cannot overestimate the effect of a setting, facing Snowdon across the broad Vale of Clwyd and overlooking smaller valleys like that of the Elwy, which provided rich emblems for expressing and activating all that he had intellectually decided upon. It called freshly, and in another country, to his natural capacity for Praise.

Throughout even 'The Wreck of the Deutschland' Hopkins took much of his theological bearings and his power of imaginative advocacy from natural imagery — images of mountain waters, stars, rivers, wild fruit and 'pied and peeled May' as well as their darker counterpart in the murdering snow-storm that wrecked the ship. One stanza in particular distils the complex pattern of ecstatic descriptive response leading to religious insight that also marks the other, shorter poems released by the amazingly creative three years at St Beuno's:

> I kiss my hand
> To the stars, lovely-asunder
> Starlight, wafting him out of it; and
> Glow, glory in thunder;
> Kiss my hand to the dappled-with-damson west:
> Since, tho' he is under the world's splendour and wonder,
> His mystery must be instressed, stressed;
> For I greet him the days I meet him, and bless when I understand.
>
> (Stanza 5)

All the hallmarks of the full poetic career are already there: the forcefully expressive yet meticulously structured form; the vitalizing response to the created world (but salted and sobered, too, in the conjoining of lovely *starlight* and challenging *thunder*); the relationship between outer-natural image and inner-religious significance, calling not only for unique perception ('instressed' – that word again) but also for tense proclamation ('stressed'); and, conveniently, the accidental expression of what is likely to be the reader's own experience in reading Hopkins – 'For I greet him the days I meet him, and bless when I understand'.

II

Bridges said that 'The Wreck of the Deutschland' stood at the entrance to Hopkins's mature poems like a dragon folded in the gate, forbidding entrance.[9] It is certainly true that works of smaller compass provide easier access. Hopkins's most characteristic form is in any case the sonnet – though it is a form made to carry more than its obvious weight and cargo, through a verbal resourcefulness unique in English poetry. And in the end the essential nature of the longer poem is faithfully epitomized in that of the shorter ones. Any new reader would therefore do well to move first from the individual stanza from 'The Wreck of the Deutschland' quoted above to the sonnets written during 1877, Hopkins's third year at St Beuno's. These include 'God's Grandeur', 'The Starlight Night', 'Pied Beauty' and 'Hurrahing in Harvest'. They distil the joy and certainty which marked the resumption of Hopkins's career as a poet and out of which arose his positive response even to the tragedy of the *Deutschland*. Their number would clearly have been greater if Hopkins had been granted, as he himself desired, an extra fourth year of study at St Beuno's.

Let us take, and retain, as our point of departure and reference in characterizing the nature of Hopkins's poetry the most celebrated of those poems of 1877 – 'The Windhover', 'the best thing I ever wrote'. Our aim in this part of the introduction will be to describe the wider features of Hopkins's art by first of all allowing concrete examples within this specific poem to direct our attention.

The Windhover:

To Christ our Lord

I caught this morning morning's minion, king-
    dom of daylight's dauphin, dapple-dawn-drawn Falcon, in
        his riding
Of the rolling level underneath him steady air, and striding
High there, how he rung upon the rein of a wimpling wing
In his ecstasy! then off, off forth on swing,
    As a skate's heel sweeps smooth on a bow-bend: the hurl and
        gliding
    Rebuffed the big wind. My heart in hiding
Stirred for a bird, — the achieve of, the mastery of the thing!

Brute beauty and valour and act, oh, air, pride, plume, here
    Buckle! AND the fire that breaks from thee then, a billion
Times told lovelier, more dangerous, O my chevalier!

No wonder of it: shéer plód makes plough down sillion
Shine, and blue-bleak embers, ah my dear,
    Fall, gall themselves, and gash gold-vermilion.

The first point worth making about such a poem concerns the
irreducible integrity of its ostensible subject. From the start,
the dense texture (and in this case also the sub-title dedication)
dispose us to expect indirect meanings beyond the apparent.
But the poem remains decisively a minutely observed description of this particular falcon's flight, opening out in the first
place only into a generalizing ending traditional to the sonnet
form. A comment of Ezra Pound's comes to mind: 'I believe that
the proper and perfect symbol is the natural object, that if a man
uses "symbols" he must so use them that their symbolic function does not obtrude; so that *a* sense, and the poetic quality of
the passage, is not lost to those who do not understand the
symbol as such, to whom, for instance, a hawk is a hawk.'[10]
Though Pound's last words are only a coincidence (he was not
thinking of Hopkins's poem), the whole comment is crucial.
The solid reality of the world, whether the overall subject of a
poem or local image within it, is for Hopkins a presence not to
be put by. This is so despite the fact that everything is from the
start (like the world in 'God's Grandeur') 'charged' with signifi-

cance. Ironically, the irreducibility of actual things in the world was less compromised by Hopkins's theology than it was by other Victorian poets' interest in symbolic landscapes, dream atmosphere, medieval allegory, classical myth, or 'poetic' properties generally. The reality of objects is elaborated and viewed in a highly individualistic way, but it is not easily removed, and does not simply 'stand for' something else. In this way, the classical symbolism of the sonnet 'Andromeda' (1879), allegorizing the poet's sense of the Victorian church beset by its enemies, is uncharacteristic. Yet Hopkins's avowed aim of avoiding mere 'quaintness'[11] in that sonnet, through its irresistibly concrete realization, shows the same respect for the independent reality of things.

Indeed, 'thing' or 'things' is a big word in Hopkins: 'These things, these things were here and but the beholder/Wanting' ('Hurrahing in Harvest'), or 'Each mortal thing does one thing and the same' ('As kingfishers catch fire') and here also in 'The Windhover' — 'the achieve of, the mastery of the thing!' That denaturing word, however, only puts into relief the central aim of a Hopkins poem, which is to raise 'things' to the level of phenomena, with the force of revelation rather than mere assertion. 'No wonder of it': what the last three lines of 'The Windhover' realize and make real is the ability of ordinary things (the plough, the embers) to reflect a glory usually associated only with agents and actions higher up the scale of creation. This is a real meaning, which directs us retrospectively to see a hierarchy of interrelated significance established in the poem as a whole: the plough and embers, the windhover in masterful flight, the suddenly ecstatic human being, and 'Christ our Lord'. The way the hierarchy sanctions the humble by association, while still remaining a hierarchy, sprang naturally from Hopkins's Roman Catholicism, and informs all the poetry. It finds clear expression in the sonnet of tribute to St Alphonsus Rodriguez, whose 'honour' was not 'flashed off exploit' but was a quiet 'conquest' in a 'world without event'. It also combines with Hopkins's stratified, and essentially Victorian, view of society in 'Tom's Garland: upon the Unemployed' and with his equally Victorian respect for the serving forces in 'Yes. Why do we all, seeing of a soldier' and 'The Bugler's First Communion'. There is more sense than one in which this Jesuit celebrates belonging to an order.

But already our interpretation reveals something closer to the very texture and inner activity of the poetry itself. For if we are to see both the poet's 'heart in hiding' and 'Christ our Lord' celebrated at a level higher than the falcon, then both are to be identified as being addressed in these lines:

> AND the fire that breaks from thee then, a billion
> Times told lovelier, more dangerous, O my chevalier!

Of course, that dual reference is easily accommodated, and meaningful: if the bird is beautiful, how much more beautiful is Christ; and also how much more beautiful the act of ecstatic recognition in a human perceiver. But the point is that a deeper association of meanings is at work than either of these readings, left like that, would allow. We can gauge it by thinking again of the images of plough and embers in the final lines. What they have in common is the irony that it is the experience of resistance and breakage that makes them shine and flame. It is the harrowing encounter of plough and hard earth that makes both shine, and the fact is intensified in the *fall gall* and *gash* that breaks the blue-bleak embers into vermilion flame. This retrospectively activates a more challenging meaning in the preceding lines, and throws us back to the word 'Buckle!' The insistence of the words 'Brute beauty', 'air', 'pride' and 'plume' also enables us to retain the falcon itself as the thing addressed. The poet has in fact seen two aspects of the bird in flight. At one moment, its controlling mastery; at another, the bird momentarily stopped and broken in the very act of rebuffing the big wind ('buckled', spreadeagled, crucified on the wind?). It is probably *that* experience which Hopkins at the deepest level describes as 'a billion times told lovelier', and significantly 'more dangerous'. Of course, the martial imagery and the sheer energy of the poem (jointly reflecting the zeal of the new Jesuit) provide other connotative meanings for 'Buckle!': for example, the sense of 'buckling on armour' or 'buckling down' to a deed. But we suddenly realize that the sense of being under stress, and broken, is more deeply in league with the emphasis of the sestet. Hopkins's poetry is enriched by multiple references. His language is excitable as well as exciting, suggestible as well as suggestive; but it still calls for adjudication as to which meanings have priority. The fuller realization, therefore, is that Christ is connotatively present in the poem not only in the princely aggrandizement of the imagery, but through the particular relevance of His greater glory in the suffering on the cross. This is a realization that also explodes in the suggestions of pain ('gall'), the spear-wound ('gash'), and blood ('vermilion') of the final line.

The word 'explode' is Hopkins's own, and points to a central characteristic of the kind of poetry we are now describing. 'One of two kinds of clearness one should have,' he wrote, 'either the meaning to be felt without effort as fast as one reads or else, if dark at first reading, when once made out *to explode*'.[12] The poetry's dense verbal and syntactic texture has a resistant power that makes the pent-up or delayed meaning all the more forceful when it comes. It may not always, as in 'The Windhover', be the dynamic, comprehensive explosion of the poem's central emphasis. Equally important is the sudden illumination of the role a local image or a series of otherwise innocent words plays within the body of a poem. When, in 'God's Grandeur', Hopkins says that 'morning, at the brown brink eastward, springs' the appropriateness of the verb is not immediately apparent. Dawn is not usually thought of as 'springing', even though the poetical word 'dayspring' is relevant here. But another force in the word 'springs' is released in conjunction with a line a little further back: 'There lives the dearest freshness deep down things'. Originally abstract assertion, that line is now given the association of 'springs' of water. The fact that the two lines in question are linked by rhyme emphasizes that we need to reconsider what we normally describe as rhyme. For, deeper than the chiming of 'springs' and 'things', is the consonance of the two lines at this, more subliminal level. A reader of 'The

Lantern out of Doors' will likewise sense a tension between the two uses of the word 'interest', at the beginning and at the end of that poem. The movement from something that 'interests our eyes' to 'Christ's interest' will suddenly be revealed as a careful deepening of the financial-redemptive meaning of the word, via other words like 'rare', 'rich' and 'buys'. The poetry is zealously self-referential in ways which explode even the most casual words into significance. Indeed, perhaps 'implosion' (a word not yet coined in Hopkins's day: it would have taken Hopkins to coin it) would be a more accurate description. The language is constantly being directed inwards to create new possibilities within the close community of the words rather than outwards to create a predetermined atmosphere or a paraphraseable statement or broad narrative. Bearing in mind Shakespeare's great soliloquies, one might speak of this as the difference between a Shakespearean and a Spenserian use of language. Within Hopkins's own period, the contrast is with the more loosely decorative side of the poetic influence of Keats on the Victorians, and to which Hopkins's own early poems had more slavishly fallen prey. The mature poetry is more strenuously concerned to give each word its full functional part in the creation of meaning. Consider the phrase 'dapple-dawn-drawn Falcon' in 'The Windhover'. The bird is attracted by the dawn, certainly; but it is also pictorially 'drawn', being outlined vividly against the dawn light. And we suddenly realize that it is a poet who was also an artist who is here claiming to have 'caught', or captured, the essence of the bird's flight.

This capturing of the essential reality of a thing became central to the poetry. It is something the poems formulate and state, as well as illustrate or act out. Its formulation is conveniently there in yet another meaning demanded by the verb 'Buckle!' in 'The Windhover'. Culminating as it does the series of six nouns from 'Brute beauty' to 'plume', it suggests (or urges) that these qualities of the bird's flight 'buckle' or connect together to make one unique event. This leads us to the phenomena (philosophical, religious, graphic and poetic) which Hopkins termed 'inscape' and 'instress'. And in this connection it is necessary to outline the various influences and natural tendencies which dovetailed and matured in Hopkins's mind in the period leading up to the recommencement of his career as a mature poet in 1875.

Central to everything is an almost obsessive delight in graphic detail. The early diaries (1863–66) and the journals (1866–75) are accumulatively characterized by descriptions and drawings which seek to isolate and understand the minute details of such things as church architecture, cloud formations, water coming through a lock, a particular sunrise or sunset, plants, trees and flowers. In a letter of 1863 Hopkins wrote:

> . . . for a certain time I am astonished at the beauty of a tree, shape, effect etc, then when the passion, so to speak, has subsided, it is consigned to my treasury of explored beauty, and acknowledged with admiration and interest ever after, while something new takes its place in my enthusiasm. The present fury is the ash, and perhaps barley and two shapes of growth in leaves and one in tree boughs and also a conformation of fine-weather clouds.[13]

Such details are most often isolated from their wider contexts, and vague feelings of the 'picturesque' play no part in their appeal. It is worth remembering that close scientific-botanical interest came itself to a fine flowering in Victorian England. Again, Ezra Pound's witty reference to the Pre-Raphaelite painter who was doing a twilight scene but rowed across the river in day time to see the shape of the leaves on the further bank, which he then drew in with full detail, reminds us of another pictorial context that makes Hopkins's tendency characteristic of his time. More correctly parallel and influential, however, was Ruskin's intellectual attention in *Modern Painters* to the 'laws' which governed the distinctive configurations of such things as fronds or clouds, the shapes of trees, or the symmetry of a chestnut fan. The verbal descriptions in the journals and, on a different scale, the drawings also remind us of that 'urge to know' that we see in Leonardo da Vinci's private drawings, and which has always been part of an artist's attempt to understand the patterns of physical reality. Hopkins's scientific interest even caused him to write letters to *Nature*, detailing the colour changes seen in sunsets as affected by the Krakatoa eruption of 1883.

But this natural interest served something more than pictorialism or quietly objective understanding. It will be clear already, for example, that conceptual qualities ('beauty', 'valour', 'pride') come together with the physical in creating that particular moment in which things 'buckle' together in the windhover's flight; that the perceiver as well as the perceived is involved; that the sense of a unique event is communicated, in which a fire of recognition illuminates understanding. A reader with knowledge of the 'spots of time' in Wordsworth's *Prelude*, of the effect of 'epiphanies' in James Joyce's work, or of the 'timeless moments' ('the intersection of the timeless with time') in T. S. Eliot's *Four Quarters*, will be within reach of the kind of experience that informed so much of Hopkins's thinking. But the exact nature of Hopkins's experience remains individual enough for him to have had to coin the words 'inscape' and 'instress' for his purposes.

From its first use in a notebook of 1868, 'inscape' varies in its emphasis, but its main reference is to the distinctive pattern of a thing. The very source of the coinage (by analogy with 'landscape') emphasizes the relationship of parts to the whole, suggesting the integrity of that whole: 'All the world is full of inscape, and chance left free to act falls into an order as well as purpose.'[14] The coinage links the word very strongly to the visual appearance of things, and demands as much recognition for the complex design of the smallest item as for the relationship of items in a larger scene, emphasizing the uniqueness of both, and their changing uniqueness at particular times. When W. B. Yeats in 'Among Schoolchildren' asks

> O chestnut tree, great-rooted blossomer,
> Are you the leaf, the blossom or the bole?

he means to resist the notion that things are only an aggregate, a mechanical sum-total, of their parts. That celebration of the irreducible completeness of a living thing is relevant here, too, but Hopkins pursues it more strenuously to the point of much more individual visual recognition. A sense of outrage at the injury done to nature by industrialism in Victorian England, expressed in 'God's Grandeur' and 'The Sea and the Skylark', was something he shared with more public contemporaries like Matthew Arnold and William Morris; but Hopkins focuses on particular rather than general loss. The 'strokes of havoc' which in 1879 felled the 'Binsey Poplars' at Oxford *'unselve/*The sweet *especial* scene'. At Roehampton six years earlier, an ash tree was felled: 'seeing it maimed there came at that moment a great pang and I wished to die and not see the inscapes of the world destroyed any more'.[15] No two things, even of the same kind, are identical. Each individual loss is irreplaceable. The key-note of 'inscape' is not only pattern, but *unique* pattern.

'Instress' is the term which explains why 'inscape' was no simple conservationist-aesthetic matter for Hopkins. Though the two words are sometimes used interchangeably, 'instress' describes essentially the active energy which binds things or parts into these unique relationships. Though it played no part in Hopkins's coinage of the word, we might momentarily fix as its opposite the notion of *'dis*tress', whose root meaning is the sense of falling apart, of incoherence. The integrating quality or action of 'instress' Hopkins saw as being the creative energy of God, actively working in the world. In his very first use of the word in the journals, describing the philosophy of Parmenides, he writes that 'all things are upheld by instress and are meaningless without it'.[16] But it is also a faculty of the human mind, which can itself bring things into creative relationship. As such, it demands an act of pure attention, dependent on solitary meditation, for 'with a companion the eye and the ear are for the most part shut and instress cannot come'.[17] Just as the prefix *in* emphasizes again the inwardness involved, the word *stress* emphasizes the tension (what Hopkins elsewhere calls the 'stalling'[18]) which holds things in that distinctive relationship which comprises the 'inscape' of the whole.

Ideas concerning the apprehension of pattern and harmony, relayed and modified through medieval philosophy from the various formulations of Plato and Aristotle, are central to

Western aesthetic thought. They form a context not to be ignored in seeking to understand Hopkins's particular vision. Thus Thomas Aquinas, whose teaching the Jesuits were generally urged to follow, speaks of three aspects of the nature of beauty: *integritas*, the quality of an object as an entity discrete from other entities: *consonantia*, the inner harmony of the related parts constituting that object: and *claritas*, the brightness or radiance of the object. But an important philosophical emphasis marks Hopkins off from Aquinas. We can approach the essential difference through Stephen Daedalus's analysis of Aquinas's terms in James Joyce's *Stephen Hero*:

Now for the third quality. For a long time I couldn't make out what Aquinas meant. He uses a figurative word (a very unusual thing for him) but I have solved it. *Claritas* is *quidditas*. After the analysis which discovers the second quality [the *consonantia*] the mind makes the only logically possible synthesis and discovers the third quality. This is the moment which I call epiphany. First we recognize that the object is *one* integral thing, then we recognize that it is an organized composite structure, a *thing* in fact: finally, when the relation of the parts is exquisite, when the parts are adjusted to the special point, we recognize that it is *that* thing which it is. Its soul, its whatness, leaps to us from the vestment of its appearance. The soul of the commonest object, the structure of which is so adjusted, seems to us radiant. The object achieves its epiphany.

'When the parts are adjusted to the special point, we recognize that it is *that* thing which it is': the two halves of that sentence come close to defining, respectively, 'instress' and 'inscape'. But Stephen's excited stress on individuality is closer to Hopkins than it is to Aquinas and would find its philosophical validation, not in Aquinas, but in the work of the British medieval philosopher and Franciscan Friar, Duns Scotus. It was indeed in Scotus that Hopkins found just that validation for what was already a spontaneous aspect of his way of seeing the world. At St Mary's seminary, Stonyhurst, six years after the commencement of his journal and three years before the recommencement of his poetry, a journal entry reads: 'At this time I had first begun to get hold of the copy of Scotus on the

Sentences in the Baddely library and was flush with a new stroke
of enthusiasm. It may come to nothing or it may be a mercy
from God. But just then when I took in any inscape of the sky or
sea I thought of Scotus.'[19] Scotus also appealed to Hopkins as a
passionate advocate of the doctrine of the Immaculate Conception of Mary, and because of his belief that Christ's Incarnation
was predestined irrespective of any reparation for human sin.
But it was Scotus's theory of knowledge that caused this 'new
stroke of enthusiasm'. Aquinas, and the Schoolmen generally,
placed the emphasis on the recognition of those aspects of a
thing which related it to a universal category. Although they
conceded that all knowledge starts in the senses, what that
knowledge meant for them was a recognition of the general
classes of reality to which individual things belonged, and
which alone allowed us to make intellectual sense of particulars
(*particulare sentitur; universale intelligitur*). But Scotus argued
that it is already a feature of the general category itself to make
the individual thing distinctive. Our knowledge, then, is of a
particular, not a general, reality. Our knowledge is, to use
Scotus's own term, of the 'haecceitas', the *thisness* of a thing —
and not simply of the 'quidditas', or the *whatness*, of its universal
form or category. Hopkins seized on the emphasis, not as
confirming merely the endless variety of the created world, but
as emphasizing that everything reveals its own ideal self *because*,
rather than in spite of, its particularity. Hopkins's note at the
head of his sonnet to Henry Purcell praises that composer
because he 'uttered in notes the very make and species of man as
created both in him and in all men generally'. Beyond the
distinctive beauties of the natural world, celebrated in sonnets
like 'Pied Beauty', 'As kingfishers catch fire' and the one on
'Duns Scotus's Oxford', the distinctiveness of the human individual becomes even more important, and a greater responsibility, because the ideal reflected in him is the distinctiveness
incarnate in Christ.

The responsibility of realizing, making real, the unique
example of Christ was patterned for every Jesuit in the *Spiritual
Exercises* of St Ignatius Loyola. Its four parts or 'Weeks' (the

purgation of past sins; contemplation of the Life of Christ and an Election to follow God's will; meditation on Christ's Passion; and on the Resurrection) had been central to Hopkins's formal training from the start of his novitiate period in September 1868, and remained the pattern of study, meditation and practice of his whole career. The inscaping of Christ's glory-through-suffering in Hopkins's experience of the windhover's flight ('Buckle! AND the fire that breaks from thee then . . .'), or in his experience of the wreck of the *Deutschland*, have also the disciplined meditation of the *Spiritual Exercises* behind them. This bringing home of the individual reality of Christ to the individual mind of man, along with the unique identities of nature, and the distinctions and distinctiveness of language, is the disciplined concern of the whole career. The particular way in which Hopkins reflected that discipline is marked above all else by his belief that the sensational world of unique events and unique identities is experienced by unique *perceivers*. Thus, of the uncompleted commentary on the *Spiritual Exercises* which Hopkins started writing in 1880, the most relevant to a study of the poetry is that on the 'First Principle and Foundation', which precedes the first 'Week'. St Ignatius's opening injunction, 'Man was created to praise', underlines all of Hopkins's work. But in his commentary he halts with '*Homo creatus est*', and his thoughts on the logical evidence that man *is* a created being, not an accident or something merely 'self existent', turn on what he calls a 'feeling of myself, that taste of myself, of *I* and *me* above and in all things'. Since human nature is more highly distinctive even than other things in the world, it cannot have been arbitrarily 'evolved, condensed, from the vastness of the world': it can only have been created by 'one of finer or higher pitch and determination than itself'. It is here that Hopkins's naturally individuating, or Scotist, tendency fuses with the Loyolan duties of his calling: in recognizing that the uniqueness of his own sensibility is at the service of proof and praise. 'I find myself both as man and as myself something most determined and distinctive, at pitch, more distinctive and higher pitched than anything else I see'.[20]

Determined, *distinctive*, *at pitch*: nothing better illustrates this feel-of-self than the irresistible need he also felt to find only the most nearly exact expression for it, by considering anew the rhythmic and verbal resources of the language. '. . . as air, melody, is what strikes me most of all in music, and design in painting, so design, pattern or what I am in the habit of calling "inscape" is what I above all aim at in poetry'.[21] Just as instress is what brings inscape into focus, the instressing element which emphasizes the different local inscapes of the poetry, and holds them in a particular overall tension, is the special kind of *movement* that Hopkins achieves in his verse. To that movement he gave the name 'Sprung Rhythm'. Its character and individual power will already have been felt in the reader's experience of 'The Windhover'. It had had its first and fullest manifestation two years before in 'The Wreck of the Deutschland': 'I had long had haunting my ear the echo of a new rhythm which I now realized on paper.'[22] The lectures on problems of rhythm, metre and prosody delivered during his year's teaching at Manresa House, Roehampton, directly before he went to St Beuno's, had formed a background to Hopkins's questioning of what can be done with the pace, stress and movement of verse.

The common rhythm of traditional English poetry — what Hopkins called 'Standard' or 'Running' Rhythm — can be measured in feet of either two or three syllables. Those of two syllables can be either iambic ($\cup-$) or trochaic ($-\cup$); those of three syllables either anapaestic ($\cup\cup-$) or dactylic ($-\cup\cup$). But of course irregular effects can happen at the beginning or the end of lines, either before the main pattern has got into its stride, or after it has already been established in the line. Hopkins himself also drew attention to some unusual metrical units, even in 'Standard Rhythm', in which feet can appear to be paired together, thus allowing double or composite feet to arise. A more obvious truth is that any poetry with real rhythmic life, as opposed to metronomic regularity, will in any case cloud or mix the basic pattern from time to time. For example, the most common pattern of English verse, the iambic, will often have its notional regularity cut across, not only by variations, but also by the natural pressure and demands of the spoken voice. A kind of counterpoint therefore develops – between the basic pattern and the variations, and between the basic pattern and the demands of natural speech.

Already, then, we see that regularity leaves room for irregularity. But Sprung Rhythm is not a simple capitalization on this fact. Hopkins himself often adopts a 'Standard' rhythm (the iambic pentameter of the sonnet, for example) and then counterpoints it:

> The world is charged with the grandeur of God.
>   It will flame out, like shining from shook foil;
>   It gathers to a greatness, like the ooze of oil
> Crushed. Why do men then now not reck his rod?
> Generations have trod, have trod, have trod . . .

Here, the basic iambic pentameter is perceptible as a ghost-presence underneath the variations mounted upon it, or set in counterpoint to it, by the freer spoken voice. This could of course lead to a stage where the underlying pattern isn't perceived at all, where we have a sense, not of counterpoint, but of uncompromised natural speech. Some of the poems of John Donne would be good examples. But neither case is a case of Sprung Rhythm. Donne, for example, like Hopkins in 'God's Grandeur' above, accepts a regular count of syllables per line. And the first thing that Sprung Rhythm is, is a rejection of that principle.

'To speak shortly, it consists in scanning by accents or stress alone, without any account of the number of syllables, so that a foot may be one strong syllable, or it may be many light and one strong.'[23] In such a scheme, as not in 'Standard' rhythm, a foot can vary from one to four syllables. And Hopkins went further. He allowed himself the freedom to add to any foot what he calls 'hangers' or 'outriders'. These are one, two, or three syllables which are not counted in the official metre: 'not part of it, not being counted, but part of it by producing a calculated effect which tells in the general success'.[24] Therefore for particular rhythmic effects Sprung Rhythm allows, more freely than common rhythm, the use of any number of slack syllables, predetermined only by the poet's ear. The two principles at the heart of Sprung Rhythm, then, are: first, its complete removal of a traditional metrical pattern which we might identify as 'iambic' or 'trochaic' etc; and then a freedom (limited only by the ear, but certainly limited) in deciding the number of syllables per line. Another aspect is what Hopkins calls 'overreaving'; that is to say, the effect whereby the scansion of one line continues that of the preceding line. Thus 'if the first has one or more syllables at its end the other must have so many the less at its beginning; and in fact the scanning runs on without a break from the beginning, say, of a stanza to the end and all the stanza is one long strain, though written in lines asunder'.[25] The opening lines of 'The Windhover' are a good example. It could even be claimed that in the Sprung Rhythm sonnets the metrical unit is not any individual lines or sections but the movement of the complete whole.

Hopkins had to add a varied complement of markings to denote the special requirements of unusual stresses, elisions, or pauses. At one stage he even argued the possibility of adding markings to denote the *syntactic* status of words in a poem – to distinguish the subject, verb, object, and indicate the general grammatical construction to the eye. Even with metrical markings, few would feel confident of an ability to scan each poem perfectly; and even Hopkins himself agreed that, in any case, metre is not an exact science. Sprung Rhythm, like any other, depends for example on the individual's pronunciation of words. 'Do you think all had best be left to the reader?'[26] he once asked; and indeed increasing familiarity with the verse makes the reader feel that rationalized, metrical validation is not a crucial necessity. The length of lines may sometimes surprise, but no line is rhythmically such a monstrosity as to make such validation necessary. Why, then, should Sprung Rhythm be worth describing at all?

The answer is that it is the corner-stone of our understanding of the *kind* of poet Hopkins is in technical matters. In effect, he is a paradox. He chose to free himself from inherited rules, but no poet has ended off being a more strenuous formalist. As in everything else, he felt that submitting to rules was a test of strength which would produce greater deliverance, and deliver more, than would otherwise be possible. But in the area of prosody and form, as nowhere else in the disciplines that committed him, he could make those rules himself, in league only with the genius of the language. The first emphasis therefore falls on the *discipline* of that which he achieved. Bridges compared 'The Leaden Echo and the Golden Echo' to the poetry of Walt Whitman, but Hopkins refused comparison with the more genuinely free-wheeling verse of the American: 'For that piece of mine is very highly wrought. The long lines are not rhythm run to seed: everything is weighed and timed in them.'[27] It is not surprising therefore to find signs of that calculated base to what appears spontaneous reflected in other ways as well. Take the opening of 'The Starlight Night':

> Look at the stars! look, look up at the skies!
>   O look at all the fire-folk sitting in the air!
>   The bright boroughs, the circle-citadels there!
> Down in dim woods the diamond delves! the elves'-eyes!
> The grey lawns cold where gold, where quickgold lies!
>   Wind-beat whitebeam! airy abeles set on a flare!
>   Flake-doves sent floating forth at a farmyard scare!

The images have been arranged in alphabetical sequence — *a* to *g*, but with *f* and *g* reversed. Or consider Hopkins's meticulous play with vowel qualities, involving not just simple assonance but the running of vowels up a scale determined by their pronunciation in the mouth. In 'The Sea and the Skylark' for example:

> Left hand, off land, I hear the lark ascend

or in 'To R. B.':

> The rise, the roll, the carol, the creation.

Such effects, like Sprung Rhythm itself, tie that which appears spontaneous and casual to a discipline of pattern and measurement. Technique which required hard labour removed poetry from easy indulgence. It united the private with the 'given', art with craft, the poet with the priest. No wonder of it: sheer plod makes plough down sillion shine. When we pay to Hopkins's poetry that praise he gave to Purcell's music — 'it is the rehearsal/Of own, of abrupt self there so thrusts on, so throngs the ear' — we must salute not only the abrupt expressiveness but the 'rehearsal' which sets it unchangeably in order.

But the enthusiastic abruptness also has its claims: Hopkins said that by 'sprung' he meant 'abrupt'. The attraction of Sprung Rhythm was essentially not the accumulative expansiveness afforded by extra syllables but the abrupt juxtaposition of stresses it allowed by recognizing even a single stress, on its own, as a complete foot. 'For why', he asked, 'if it is forcible in prose to say "lashed: rod", am I obliged to weaken this in verse, which ought to be stronger, not weaker, into "láshed birch-ród" or something?'[28] He recognized that English is naturally a stressed language. Though Sprung Rhythm had precedents in a variety of literatures (ancient Greek drama, the Odes of Pindar, Hebrew Psalms, as well as Old English alliterative verse, nursery rhymes, late Shakespeare, late Milton and Coleridge's 'Christabel') it was doubtless the dramatically expressive force of the English language itself that Hopkins was harnessing. Other possibilities rich in that language — assonance and alliteration patterned even more scrupulously through Hopkins's emulation of the poetic effects of *cynghanedd*[29] in Welsh, a language he learned at St Beuno's) or the force of compound phrases or of dialect words and idioms — all these are put at stress, energized, and precipitated by the 'abrupt' or 'spring' movement.

In a letter to Mowbray Baillie in 1864, Hopkins wrote that the language of poetry can be divided into three kinds.[30] The third and lowest — that which defines verse as distinct from prose — he only briefly mentions. His first two categories, however, reflect on the logic behind the kind of sharpened distinctiveness that his own poetry was to attempt. His second category, defining the threshold of excellence as he saw it, he termed 'Parnassian':

It can only be spoken by poets, but it is not in the highest sense poetry. It does not require the mood of mind in which the poetry of inspiration is written. It is spoken *on and from the level* of a poet's mind, not, as in the other case, when the inspiration which is the gift of genius, raises him above himself . . . Great men, poets I mean, have each their own dialect as it were of Parnassian, formed generally as they go on writing, and at last, – this is the point to be marked, – they can see things in this Parnassian way and describe them in this Parnassian tongue, without further effort of inspiration. In a poet's particular kind of Parnassian lies most of his style, of his manner, of his mannerism if you like.

The thing about Parnassian is that the reader can imagine himself writing it if he were the poet, though Hopkins concedes that whether one *could* write it is another matter. This possibility of identification is what causes a poet to pall on us, as Wordsworth palls ('We seem to have found out his secret'), or as Tennyson comes to be thought merely 'Tennysonian'. Hopkins interestingly defines an extra category – 'Castalian' – 'a higher sort of Parnassian'. The point about Castalian is that one cannot conceive having written it, but it remains nevertheless too 'characteristic' of the poet, 'too so-and-so-all-overish'.

One might be tempted to say that that ultimate refinement of the highly 'characteristic' embraces also Hopkins's own work. If we are not to leave it at that, much depends on Hopkins's definition of his highest category:

The first and highest is poetry proper, the language of inspiration. The word inspiration need cause no difficulty. I mean by it a mood of great, abnormal in fact, mental acuteness, either energetic or passive, according as the thoughts which arise in it seem generated by a stress and action of the brain, or to strike into it unasked . . . In a fine piece of inspiration every beauty takes you as it were by surprise . . . every fresh beauty could not in any way be predicted or accounted for by what one has already read.

There is clearly a quality of overstatement in that last sentence. It appears to speak of style with minimum recognition of the necessarily incremental way in which poems or passages create the taste by which they are to be enjoyed and recognized as total entities. There might even appear to be something precious about phrases like 'a fine piece of inspiration', 'every beauty', 'every fresh beauty'. Just as within Parnassian Hopkins would anthologize, looking for the stroke of 'inspiration', so within the poetry of 'inspiration' itself he would anthologize further and claim for every surprise, every fresh beauty, a quality that could 'not in any way be predicted or accounted for by what one has already read'. But however decadent this might appear out of the context later provided by the achievement of his own poems, its actual logic is already that of the poet of tireless inscapes. More generally, it seems to partake of the Keatsian notion of 'loading every rift with ore'. This would also of course beg the question raised in Coleridge's assertion that 'a poem of any length neither can be, or ought to be, all poetry'.[31] Coleridge would have seen Parnassian as being that lower level of (still mastered) style which necessarily has to act as vehicle for the greater intensities and inspirations that one tends to want to call poetry itself, what Hopkins calls 'poetry proper'. 'The Wreck of the Deutschland' would appear to belie the belief that no 'poem of any length' can be full of poetry, defined in these terms of intensity of inspiration; but it remains significant that Hopkins never attempted anything as capacious again, and that the main formal emphasis of his career seems to have been on redefining what the shorter sonnet form can be made to accommodate.

For Hopkins aims, with an unusual consistency, at a sustained level of intensity. In this, his situation and his art again came together. It is as if the excitement which published poetry creates beyond itself, in its audience, had in this private case to be more immediately guaranteed, more copiously prefigured, and sustained, in the tension of the verse itself. The point about Hopkins's output is that it was not in the ordinary sense 'put out'. To appropriate a line from a poem by Auden, 'he became his admirers'. Hopkins illustrated as much when he told Bridges 'You are my audience' and then proceeded, in the main, to ignore even Bridges's expectations as to what poetry should or should not do. To the service of this increased intensity came his natural belief in the possibility of infinite riches in a little room (within the sonnet, within the image, within even the individual word, relished for its many and simultaneous possibilities). It is in the context of this notion of rich containment that the relative smallness of his output and ostensible range has also to be seen. The question his poetry raises is whether that intensity becomes, as Donald Davie put it, 'a muscle-bound monstrosity', 'self-expression at its most relentless', a means 'for the individual will to impose itself on time'.[32] Such a view would have disappointed Hopkins's sense of Christian modesty even more than it would have confirmed the technical fear that went along with his enterprise: 'it is the virtue of design, pattern, or inscape to be distinctive and it is the vice of distinctiveness to become queer'.[33] If the poetry leads us back only to a sense of imposed will, it remains as deadlocked in the personal as the less adventurous Parnassian, however little we could conceive of ourselves writing it. The final court of appeal is each reader's experience of the poems. What seems clear from Hopkins's definition of the poetry of 'inspiration', however, is that he could himself imagine much better motives and much better results. At their heart would be, finally, a sense of impersonality: 'a mood of great, abnormal in fact, mental acuteness, either energetic or receptive, according as the thoughts which arise in it seem generated by a stress and action of the brain, or to strike into it unasked'. The interesting thing about the letter to Baillie is that the word 'language' does not simply denote 'diction' but the nature of poetic insight when it strikes us with a sense of suddenly discovered inevitability. Hopkins's own poetry of course came out of highly individual states of emotion. It also involved taking strenuous possession of the language. But a level of impersonality paradoxically inheres in so actively 'finding out' (more in Hopkins's sense now, of 'fetching out') language's own independent 'secrets'. It involves a view of language not as vehicle but as one of the realities of the world.

> Poetry is speech framed for contemplation of the mind by the way of hearing or speech framed to be heard for its own sake and interest even over and above its interest of meaning. Some matter and meaning is essential to it but only as an element necessary to

support and employ the shape which is contemplated for its own sake.[34]

Our century, in which criticism has decisively placed more emphasis on a poem's independent relationship to the reader ('framed for contemplation') than on its confessional relationship to the poet, would also seem equipped to see in that last statement by Hopkins something more serious than a view of art for art's sake as usually conceived.

III

An ordinary literalness underlies the usual claim that Hopkins's poetry was ahead of its time: only 'ahead of its time', belatedly in 1918, was critical appreciation on any scale even made possible. The qualitative praise that the description is meant to carry also involves a paradox, given that so much in his theology and his exploration of language went back in time for its validation and incentives. Similarly, there is so much that also marks the man himself as being clearly of his *own* time. Commenting on the battle of Majuba Hill in the war with the Boers in 1881, he lamented what he took to be British cowardice in the face of an outnumbered enemy: 'The effect will, I am afraid, be felt all over the empire.'[35] His patriotic Englishness even separated him from his fellow Jesuits in his bitter regret at the agitation for Home Rule in Ireland in the 1880s. Again, the central part played by the world of nature in the language of his sensibility reminds us that the Victorians shared the nineteenth century with the Romantics, whereas so much of twentieth-century Modernist poetry (early Eliot for example) cut off that appeal to nature, partly as a reaction against its irrelevant survival in the work of the 'Georgian' poets. In any case, it was only after the first inroads of Modernism in English poetry had already been made that Hopkins was published: late enough for his technical influence to count not with Eliot and Pound or the late Yeats, but with the poets of the 'thirties. Moreover, with both the first and second English Modernist generations of our century (that of Eliot and that of Auden) the ultimate substance of Hopkins's vision would have been in marked contrast. Poets like Yeats and Eliot wrote out of the very disintegration of the Christian world-view that stood, conservatively complete, at the centre of Hopkins's verse; and the political and social preoccupations of the 'thirties poets meant that Hopkins's influence on them appeared isolated in technical effects, self-consciously used and often at a remove from a poem's real character. It is also true that much that has gone towards altering expression in the poetry of this century has drawn on impulses that on one view might be termed anti-poetical or anti-formal, creating a new poetic out of the prosaic, the casually ironic, and the understated, and involving 'the breaking of forms' in ways very different from any recognized by Hopkins himself. In contrast, any low-key reference or association in a Hopkins poem (carrier pigeons in the third stanza of the 'Deutschland', for example, or tram rails in 'The Candle Indoors', or the outrageous rhymes of 'The Loss of the Eurydice' and 'The Bugler's First Communion') are galvanized and level-led upwards by the essentially formal energy of the verse. He remains, *par excellence*, the poet of high-definition performance.

The feeling that we read him as we read the moderns therefore brings up the question as to what it is that makes Hopkins transcend his own time and appear so attractive to ours. Does it, in the light of what has been said so far, have anything to do with his evincing an essentially modern sensibility? In any answer, his religion cannot be simply set aside. It is interesting, for example, that its dogmatic-doctrinal emphasis caused T. S. Eliot to define Hopkins as a 'devotional' rather than a 'religious' poet.[36] Eliot argued that the latter kind works on a wider range of human experience in the world than was open to Hopkins. The implication is also that 'religious' denotes a necessarily tentative awareness of the numinous and ineffable, in the face of which human decision, even language itself, loses assertive confidence. This is the sense in which Eliot's *The Waste Land* is no less 'religious' than his specifically Anglo-Catholic *Four Quartets*. Nearer Hopkins's own subject-matter, a poet like

Edward Thomas is instructive, because of a sensibility that strikes us as being of our own time without any of the technical or procedural hallmarks of more obviously Modernist verse. Thomas's experience in 'Old Man' —

> I see and I hear nothing;
> Yet seem, too, to be listening, lying in wait
> For what I should, yet never can, remember—

might be called religious, although not concerned with matters of belief in the usual sense. The interesting thing is that Hopkins would have come back at such a view from a specifically Catholic, not just a Christian, position. He wrote to Bridges: 'You do not mean by mystery what a Catholic does. You mean an interesting uncertainty: the uncertainty ceasing interest ceases also. This happens in some things; to you in religion. But a Catholic by mystery means an incomprehensible certainty.'[37] However, if one imagines a modern audience for Hopkins's poetry, wider than readers of like belief to his, it is an audience that would probably recognize itself more instinctively in Edward Thomas's reticence and inability to draw the circle complete.

The divide is also reflected at the lower level of another kind of certainty and uncertainty. There is a sort of bold descriptive assurance that supplements Victorian poetry even when that poetry does not share Hopkins's dogmatic faith or his verbal richness, and even when its themes are ones of loss or doubt or despair. It would divide a respresentatively modern, demoralized voice like Edward Thomas's not only from Hopkins but also from Arnold's 'Dover Beach' or Tennyson's 'In Memoriam'. Even in 1912–13 Thomas Hardy's poems on the memory of his first wife are still the other side of a divide from Edward Thomas. Hardy recovers lost scenes with confident clarity and fullness, whereas the very point about 'Old Man' is the existential unreality created by time. The point is that Hopkins's 'incomprehensible certainty' on a theological level bears a relationship to a more ordinary kind of certainty: for him, the world is very tangibly available to description. The way in which

Hopkins takes possession of the natural world makes Edward Thomas again an instructive contrast. In his poem 'Glory' Thomas asks a question that would, notionally, match the enterprise of Hopkins's verse:

> Shall I now this day
> Begin to seek as far as heaven, as hell,
> Wisdom or strength to match this beauty?

But the inner philosophical blankness leaves a gap between him and the beauties of the natural world, which in turn seem threatening to remain mere existential facts. He sees, but ultimately cannot *feel*, how beautiful they are: 'I cannot bite the day to the core'. That metaphor of penetrating appetite and taste is of course supremely relevant to Hopkins. In 'Hurrahing in Harvest' he *is* seen to 'Down all that glory in the heavens to glean our Saviour', and in the 'Deutschland' the intellectual recognition of Christ's presence as a fact in time is communicated through that very experience of biting to the core, with a classic archness that lies outside the idiom of our own time:

> How a lush-kept plush-capped sloe
> Will, mouthed to flesh-burst,
> Gush!
>
> (stanza 8)

And yet, ironically, it is surely this very feature that makes him seem to us so contemporaneously powerful on the one range of experience that our century, perhaps through greater psychological knowledge, is particularly able to identify and identify with. That experience is of psychic disintegration and collapse. But the power of its exploration and expression in Hopkins is not divorcible from the dynamic way in which he invades *all* experiences open to him: praise of the natural world, pastoral duty, the celebration of friends and heroes, as well as personal spiritual suffering. Everything comes down to one particular aspect of the way in which he uses language. That is his refusal to use words as simply referential tools, as signs which stand over against things, pointing to them, denoting them. In Hopkins, words *become* things — though we shall shortly have to be precise in how we define that assertion. Compared even to the heavy linguistic tangibility of Keats and the mimetic powers of Tennyson ('The long light shakes across the lakes', 'The moan of doves in immemorial elms'), Hopkins's tendency in this direction seems unique in its pitch and consistency. But its strength is in its adaptable power: for, whereas one might rightly criticize endless onomatopoeia ('As tumbled over rim in roundy wells/Stones ring') as a case of killing one bird with two stones, this way with language is also at the heart of other, deeper, effects. Language in Hopkins's hands seems intent not only on becoming things but on concretizing abstract progression in time:

> Never ask if meaning it, wanting it, warned of it – men go
> ('The Wreck of the Deutschland')

> Evening strains to be time's vast, womb-of-all, home-of-all,
> hearse-of-all night
> ('Spelt from Sibyl's Leaves')

> . . . parches
> Squandering ooze to squeezed dough, crust, dust
> ('That Nature is a Heraclitean Fire').

Its natural power, therefore, is also that of *embodying* the very movement of thought and feeling. Consider even 'Felix Randal', not the densest of the poems:

> This seeing the sick endears them to us, us too it endears.
> My tongue had taught thee comfort, touch had quenched thy tears,
> Thy tears that touched my heart, child, Felix, poor Felix Randal.

The priest's momentary self-pride in ministering to the sick is first prompted by, and then again gives way to, a more selfless love. The associative and reciprocal progress of thought and feeling there cannot be divorced from its enactment in the weight and density of the words themselves.

Without these affective powers, the poems' close textural possessiveness might deserve a reprimand drawn from Robert Graves's poem 'The Cool Web'. Graves there praises a contrary view of the offices of language: as something which coolly releases us from, rather than embroils us in, experience. 'There's a cool web of language winds us in,/Retreat from too much joy or too much fear.' If we let our tongues lose self-possession, Graves says, 'we shall go mad no doubt and die that way'. Indeed, it could be claimed that everything about Hopkins, from his journal observations of nature onwards, lives close to neurosis — to the tyranny of detail, relentless empathy, possession. A complex of factors lies behind this. At the lowest level, one might mention the taste for the 'exquisite' bred deep in his character and fed by the aesthetic and religious climate of his undergraduate days. His own frail constitution may also have sharpened his delight in the concreteness of external things. In this, balancing the attraction of the delicately 'exquisite', there is also the strong attraction of opposites: of the masterful windhover, of a world *charged* with the grandeur of God, of the muscular Harry Ploughman and the massive Felix Randal before 'sickness broke him'. Hopkins is good on dynamic subjects. But the instinctive movement from the notional and intellectual into concretely relished equivalence (rather than discursive description) in language may also have carried its own tribute to the one fact on which all his sense of reality depended: that God's Word became the world. Praise of that world through its tangible realization in words *was* praise of God.

The irony however is that the very power which makes his praise impressive (the empathic inwardness with concrete identities) made more terrible his power of feeling the stress and strain of his own identity. The Irish sonnets of desolation of 1885 manifest the extremities not only of a terrible sense of unworthiness and a bewildering sense of desertion and wastage but also of a journey to the limits of super-sensitivity, implicit in his powers from the start, and already framing the opening of the mature career in the first part of 'The Wreck of the Deutschland'. That sensitivity is in the broad tradition of Romantic poetry. In such poetry, even withdrawal from that condition becomes a theme for poems, in the form of Keats's Indolence, Coleridge's Dejection, or Wordsworth's belief that he had moved from absolute oneness with nature to the more detached moral experience of 'the still sad music of humanity'. The even greater nervous extremity of Hopkins's availability to experience is shown in the fact that withdrawal for him became a matter, not of the better conduct of his poetic career, but of the retention of sanity itself. The plea of the 'My own heart let me more have pity on' sonnet of 1885 is that he may 'live to my sad self hereafter kind'. Because of the poetic obscurity involved, we are in the presence here of a more nakedly confessional trauma than any public audience before that of our own time was used to, outside dramatic literature. But that the 1885 sonnets themselves still impose an order and provide a momentary stay against the confusion as expressed in letters ('if ever anything was written in blood, one of these was') is a consummate confirmation of that margin between neurosis and art.

For the truth is that the sonnets (to borrow Hopkins's exaggeration) were not written in blood. Words in Hopkins 'become things' in a special sense. What they most fully become is themselves. It is not so much that the poetry closes the gap between words and the things they denote as that it opens the connections between words and other words. A feeling as strong as Hopkins's of the nearly autonomous life of words compounds and reconstitutes, rather than mimes, reality. More frequent than those moments when the verse is fairly simply mimetic of an action,

> as a skate's heel sweeps smooth on a bow bend
> ('The Windhover')

or of an inner timing of responses,

> That night, that year
> Of now done darkness I wretch lay wrestling with (my God!) my God
> ('Not, I'll not, carrion comfort, Despair . . .')

— more frequent than these are the effects where the 'thinginess' of what is described has to take its place among other, wider, and often more complex reverberations released by the language. Indeed, at times the actual referent in the real world has to be very actively supplied by the reader: as in the description of the bird's song in 'The Sea and the Skylark' ('His rash-fresh re-winded new-skeined score/In crisps of curl off wild winch whirl') or the effect of light through eyelashes in 'The Candle Indoors' ('to-fro tender trambeams truckle at the eye'). It is not that the referent is slighted; quite the opposite — it is given a new order of attention in being part of a complex moment of perception, made possible not by the world but by language-and-world. The difference between more limitedly mimetic effects and this fuller verbal life can be gauged by comparing the opening of Matthew Arnold's 'Dover Beach' or W. H. Auden's 'Seaside',

> Here at the small field's ending pause
> When the chalk wall falls to the foam and its tall ledges
> Oppose the pluck
> And knock of the tide,
> And the shingle scrambles after the suck-
> ing surf

with stanza 32 of 'The Wreck of the Deutschland':

> The recurb and the recovery of the gulf's sides,
>   The girth of it and the wharf of it and the wall;
> Stanching, quenching ocean of a motionable mind;
> Ground of being, and granite of it: past all
>   Grasp God, throned behind
> Death with a sovereignty that heeds but hides, bodes but abides

In his philological examinations of possible common roots of now distinct words in his early diaries, Hopkins's main interest is certainly in words which share onomatopoeic explanations:

> The derivation of *granum*, *grain* may be referred to the head
>   *Grind*, *gride*, *gird*, *grit*, *groat*, *grate*, *greet*, κρούειν, *crush*, *crash*, κροτεῖν, etc.
>   Original meaning of *strike*, *rub*, particularly *together*. That which is produced by such means is the *grit*, the *groats* or crumbs, like *fragmentum* from *frangere*, *bit* from *bite*. *Crumb*, *crumble* perhaps akin.[38]

But it is the relationship between the words themselves that brings their mutual relationship to the world on to the level of imaginative power in the poems. Thus in the 'Deutschland' stanza just quoted, the shared sounds of 'Stanching', 'quenching' and 'ocean' certainly bring the same sound to life in 'motionable' (a coolly abstract word in any other context) and make it mime the reality. But we move to a more interesting order of revelation when we hear the reconciliation of conceptual opposites in the shared sounds of 'heeds but hides, bodes but abides'. More radical still is the reconciliation, the *fusion*, of opposites in the word 'Ground' — that which supports is also that which grinds. And the sanction for that reading comes significantly not just from the physicality that links it to the world but from the question with which the immediately preceding stanza has ended: 'is the shipwreck then a harvest, does tempest carry the *grain* for thee?' The whole effect shares in the spirit of the onomatopoeic interest of the philological notes in the diaries, but it is more significantly dominated by the images at the very opening of the poem asserting the paradox of being 'at the wall/Fast' although 'mined with a motion'. The words in the poems solidly face one another (often across many pages) as well as vertiginously facing the world. They dramatize moral reconciliations more importantly than they do realistic reproductions. Hopkins himself said that it is rhyme we admire, not echo.[39]

Most relevant of all to our sense of identification now with his experiences then is not our post-Freudian receptiveness to the literature of extremes, but something that constitutes the basic impulse in everything that he wrote. Hopkins's poetry stood out against developments in Victorian England in a deeper way than could be done by abstractly challenging its theology or lamenting the industrial ruination of its landscapes. Others, aloud in their own time, did that. It is as if, more privately than in just the obvious sense, some deep instinct drove his invasion and possession of the inner, concrete particularities of the language. A view of poetry as 'shape which is contemplated for its own sake' may seem surprising coming from a Jesuit, whose official duty it was to teach, convert and persuade. But what it makes clear is that when Hopkins resumed his poetry in 1875 he was calling to his side the very language of an England he thought misguided in its beliefs and dealings with life. Ironically, the language itself — the medium meaningfully as message — allowed him a posture for combat within the gates. This is the ultimate paradox one sets against the 'outsider' elements in his situation — his Roman Catholicism, his intensely individual sensibility, and the absence of a public audience. Moreover, he took possession of that language, not as a national outsider like Joyce or Eliot or Dylan Thomas (unconsciously changing the cultural *feel* of the language), but as one who was himself deeply English, though uniquely advantaged by having crossed so many national and regional borderlines within the British Isles. The possibility of his poetry falling out of a recognizably English idiom was his fear, not his boast. No doubt, following the language back to its roots, avoiding the standard familiarities and usages that had overlain its most naked character and its inward avenues of connection, were ways of countering the official religion that he felt had overlain his own essentially sixteenth-century Catholicism. The irreducibility of the poems, their power of simultaneous rather than serial suggestiveness, and of not outlasting their own energy, mean that, even without sharing the exact nature of his faith, we *become* Hopkins as we read. His endless insistence to Bridges that his poems should be read aloud was aimed at completing that process of indentification. But it is also as if his grappling with the inner potentialities of the language sought to defend the quality of intuitive, inward, individual life — on which alone the discriminations of good faith, of *any* kind, are made. The contemporaneity we share with him is that shared also with all great creative writers of the two centuries of industrial civilization, a civilization in which echo and easy reproduction threaten to replace rhyme and relationship, and a life lived by values. It involved respect for the secret places. The undergraduate poems had feelingly imagined these in terms of elected silence and a more total retreat:

I have desired to go
Where springs not fail,
To fields where flies no sharp and sided hail
And a few lilies blow.

And I have asked to be
Where no storms come,
Where the green swell is in the havens dumb,
And out of the swing of the sea.
(Heaven-Haven', 1864)

But in the upshot what were involved were the secret places of language, not encountered or accounted for except by opening out the very means by which we think.

Notes

1. *The Journals and Papers of G. M. Hopkins*, ed. H. House and G. Storey, 1959, p. 258.
2. 'To seem the stranger lies my lot, my life', p. 98.
3. 'Henry Purcell', p. 78.
4. *The Journals and Papers of G. M. Hopkins*, p. 165.
5. *Ibid.*, p. 71.
6. *Correspondence of G. M. Hopkins and R. W. Dixon*, ed, C. C. Abbott, 1956, p. 14.
7. *Ibid.*
8. 'I wake and feel the fell of dark, not day', p. 99.
9. Notes, *The Poems of G. M. Hopkins*, 1st edn, ed. R. Bridges, 1918.
10. 'A Retrospect', *Pavannes and Divisions*, 1918, p. 9.
11. *Letters of G. M. Hopkins to Robert Bridges*, ed. C. C. Abbott, 1955, p. 87.
12. *Ibid.*, p. 90.
13. *Further Letters of G. M. Hopkins*, ed. C. C. Abbott, 1956, p. 202.
14. *The Journals and Papers of G. M. Hopkins*, p. 230.
15. *Ibid.*
16. *Ibid.*, p. 127.
17. *Ibid.*, p. 228.
18. *Ibid.*, p. 196.
19. *Ibid.*, p. 221. The edition of Duns Scotus referred to is the *Scriptum Oxoniense super Sententiis*, 2 vols., Venice, 1514.

20. *The Sermons and Devotional Writings of G. M. Hopkins*, ed. C. Devlin S. J., 1959, pp. 122–30.
21. *Letters of G. M. Hopkins to Robert Bridges*, p. 66.
22. *Correspondence of G. M. Hopkins and R. W. Dixon*, p. 14.
23. *Ibid.*
24. *Letters of G. M. Hopkins to Robert Bridges*, p. 45.
25. 'Author's Preface': Hopkins's own description of Sprung Rythm, first published in Bridges's first edn of the poems, 1918.
26. The question was written by Hopkins on the autograph copy of 'The Leaden Echo and the Golden Echo' as sent to Bridges. He had commented that 'with the degree of stress so perpetually varying no marking is satisfactory'.
27. *Letters of G. M. Hopkins to Robert Bridges*, p. 157.
28. *Ibid.*, p. 46.
29. For a detailed examination of Hopkins's use of *cynghanedd*, see A. Llwyd, '*Cynghanedd* and English Poetry', *Poetry Wales* XIV, 1 (1978).
30. *Further Letters of G. M. Hopkins*, pp. 215–20, 221–22.
31. *Biographia Literaria*, ch. XIV.
32. 'Hopkins as a Decadent Critic', *Purity of Diction in English Verse*, 1952, pp. 160–82.
33. *Letters of G. M. Hopkins to Robert Bridges*, p. 66.
34. 'Poetry and Verse' (lecture notes), *The Journals and Papers of G. M. Hopkins*, p. 289.
35. *Further Letters of G. M. Hopkins*, p. 158.
36. 'A Note on Hopkins' in *After Strange Gods* (1934).
37. *Letters of G. M. Hopkins to Robert Bridges*, p. 186.
38. *The Journals and Papers of G. M. Hopkins*, p. 5.
39. *Ibid.*, p. 83. 'In art we strive to realize not only unity, permanence of law, likeness, but also, with it, difference, variety, contrast; it is rhyme we like, not echo, and not unison but harmony.'

THE WRECK OF THE DEUTSCHLAND

To the
happy memory of five Franciscan nuns
exiles by the Falk Laws
drowned between midnight and morning of
Dec. 7th. 1875

PART THE FIRST

1

Thou mastering me
God! giver of breath and bread;
World's strand, sway of the sea;
Lord of living and dead;
Thou hast bound bones and veins in me, fastened me flesh,
And after it almost unmade, what with dread,
Thy doing: and dost thou touch me afresh?
Over again I feel thy finger and find thee.

2

I did say yes
O at lightning and lashed rod;
Thou heardst me truer than tongue confess
Thy terror, O Christ, O God;
Thou knowest the walls, altar and hour and night:
The swoon of a heart that the sweep and the hurl of thee
trod
Hard down with a horror of height:
And the midriff astrain with leaning of, laced with fire of stress.

3

The frown of his face
Before me, the hurtle of hell

51

Behind, where, where was a, where was a place?
　　I whirled out wings that spell
And fled with a fling of the heart to the heart of the Host.
My heart, but you were dovewinged, I can tell,
　　Carrier-witted, I am bold to boast,
To flash from the flame to the flame then, tower from the grace
　　to the grace.

4

　　I am soft sift
　　In an hourglass—at the wall
Fast, but mined with a motion, a drift,
　　And it crowds and it combs to the fall;
I steady as a water in a well, to a poise, to a pane,
But roped with, always, all the way down from the tall
　　Fells or flanks of the voel, a vein
Of the gospel proffer, a pressure, a principle, Christ's gift.

5

　　I kiss my hand
　　To the stars, lovely-asunder
Starlight, wafting him out of it; and
　　Glow, glory in thunder;
Kiss my hand to the dappled-with-damson west:
Since, tho' he is under the world's splendour and wonder,
　　His mystery must be instressed, stressed;
For I greet him the days I meet him, and bless when I under-
　　stand.

6

　　Not out of his bliss
　　Springs the stress felt
Nor first from heaven (and few know this)
　　Swings the stroke dealt—
Stroke and a stress that stars and storms deliver,
That guilt is hushed by, hearts are flushed by and melt—
　　But it rides time like riding a river
(And here the faithful waver, the faithless fable and miss).

7

It dates from day
Of his going in Galilee;
Warm-laid grave of a womb-life grey;
Manger, maiden's knee;
The dense and the driven Passion, and frightful sweat;
Thence the discharge of it, there its swelling to be,
Though felt before, though in high flood yet—
What none would have known of it, only the heart, being hard
at bay,

8

Is out with it! Oh,
We lash with the best or worst
Word last! How a lush-kept plush-capped sloe
Will, mouthed to flesh-burst,
Gush!—flush the man, the being with it, sour or sweet,
Brim, in a flash, full!—Hither then, last or first,
To hero of Calvary, Christ's feet—
Never ask if meaning it, wanting it, warned of it—men go.

9

Be adored among men,
God, three-numberèd form;
Wring thy rebel, dogged in den,
Man's malice, with wrecking and storm.
Beyond saying sweet, past telling of tongue,
Thou art lightning and love, I found it, a winter and warm;
Father and fondler of heart thou hast wrung:
Hast thy dark descending and most art merciful then.

10

With an anvil-ding
And with fire in him forge thy will
Or rather, rather then, stealing as Spring
Through him, melt him but master him still:
Whether at once, as once at a crash Paul,

Or as Austin, a lingering-out sweet skill,
    Make mercy in all of us, out of us all
Mastery, but be adored, but be adored King.

PART THE SECOND

11

    'Some find me a sword; some
      The flange and the rail; flame,
    Fang, or flood' goes Death on drum,
      And storms bugle his fame.
But wé dream we are rooted in earth—Dust!
Flesh falls within sight of us, we, though our flower the
    same,
      Wave with the meadow, forget that there must
The sour scythe cringe, and the blear share come.

12

    On Saturday sailed from Bremen,
      American-outward-bound,
    Take settler and seamen, tell men with women,
      Two hundred souls in the round—
O Father, not under thy feathers nor ever as guessing
The goal was a shoal, of a fourth the doom to be drowned;
      Yet did the dark side of the bay of thy blessing
Not vault them, the million of rounds of thy mercy not reeve
    even them in?

13

    Into the snows she sweeps,
      Hurling the haven behind,
    The Deutschland, on Sunday; and so the sky keeps,
      For the infinite air is unkind,
And the sea flint-flake, black-backed in the regular blow,
Sitting Eastnortheast, in cursed quarter, the wind;

Wiry and white-fiery and whirlwind-swivellèd snow
Spins to the widow-making unchilding unfathering deeps.

14

She drove in the dark to leeward,
She struck—not a reef or a rock
But the combs of a smother of sand: night drew her
Dead to the Kentish Knock;
And she beat the bank down with her bows and the ride
of her keel:
The breakers rolled on her beam with ruinous shock;
And canvas and compass, the whorl and the wheel
Idle for ever to waft her or wind her with, these she endured.

15

Hope had grown grey hairs,
Hope had mourning on,
Trenched with tears, carved with cares,
Hope was twelve hours gone;
And frightful a nightfall folded rueful a day
Nor rescue, only rocket and lightship, shone,
And lives at last were washing away:
To the shrouds they took,—they shook in the hurling and
horrible airs.

16

One stirred from the rigging to save
The wild woman-kind below,
With a rope's end round the man, handy and brave—
He was pitched to his death at a blow,
For all his dreadnought breast and braids of thew:
They could tell him for hours, dandled the to and fro
Through the cobbled foam-fleece, what could he do
With the burl of the fountains of air, buck and the flood of the
wave?

17

They fought with God's cold—
And they could not and fell to the deck
(Crushed them) or water (and drowned them) or
    rolled
With the sea-romp over the wreck.
Night roared, with the heart-break hearing a heart-broke
    rabble,
The woman's wailing, the crying of child without check—
Till a lioness arose breasting the babble,
A prophetess towered in the tumult, a virginal tongue told.

18

Ah, touched in your bower of bone,
Are you! turned for an exquisite smart,
Have you! make words break from me here all alone,
Do you!—mother of being in me, heart.
O unteachably after evil, but uttering truth,
Why, tears! is it? tears; such a melting, a madrigal start!
Never-eldering revel and river of youth,
What can it be, this glee? the good you have there of your own?

19

Sister, a sister calling
A master, her master and mine!—
And the inboard seas run swirling and hawling;
The rash smart sloggering brine
Blinds her; but she that weather sees one thing, one;
Has one fetch in her: she rears herself to divine
Ears, and the call of the tall nun
To the men in the tops and the tackle rode over the storm's
    brawling.

20

She was first of a five and came
Of a coifèd sisterhood.
(O Deutschland, double a desperate name!

O world wide of its good!
But Gertrude, lily, and Luther, are two of a town,
Christ's lily and beast of the waste wood:
    From life's dawn it is drawn down,
Abel is Cain's brother and breasts they have sucked the same.)

21

    Loathed for a love men knew in them,
    Banned by the land of their birth,
    Rhine refused them, Thames would ruin them;
    Surf, snow, river and earth
Gnashed: but thou art above, thou Orion of light;
Thy unchancelling poising palms were weighing the worth,
    Thou martyr-master: in thy sight
Storm flakes were scroll-leaved flowers, lily showers—sweet
    heaven was astrew in them.

22

    Five! the finding and sake
    And cipher of suffering Christ.
    Mark, the mark is of man's make
    And the word of it Sacrificed.
But he scores it in scarlet himself on his own bespoken,
Before-time-taken, dearest prizèd and priced—
    Stigma, signal, cinquefoil token
For lettering of the lamb's fleece, ruddying of the rose-flake.

23

    Joy fall to thee, father Francis,
    Drawn to the Life that died;
    With the gnarls of the nails in thee, niche of the lance,
        his
    Lovescape crucified
And seal of his seraph-arrival! and these thy daughters
And five-livèd and leavèd favour and pride,
    Are sisterly sealed in wild waters,

To bathe in his fall-gold mercies, to breathe in his all-fire
      glances.

24

> Away in the loveable west,
> On a pastoral forehead of Wales,
> I was under a roof here, I was at rest,
> And they the prey of the gales;
> She to the black-about air, to the breaker, the thickly
> Falling flakes, to the throng that catches and quails
> Was calling 'O Christ, Christ, come quickly':
> The cross to her she calls Christ to her, christens her wild-worst
>   Best.

25

> The majesty! what did she mean?
> Breathe, arch and original Breath.
> Is it love in her of the being as her lover had been?
> Breathe, body of lovely Death.
> They were else-minded then, altogether, the men
> Woke thee with a *we are perishing* in the weather of Gen-
>   nesareth.
> Or is it that she cried for the crown then,
> The keener to come at the comfort for feeling the combating
>   keen?

26

> For how to the heart's cheering
> The down-dugged ground-hugged grey
> Hovers off, the jay-blue heavens appearing
> Of pied and peeled May!
> Blue-beating and hoary-glow height; or night, still higher,
> With belled fire and the moth-soft Milky Way,
> What by your measure is the heaven of desire,
> The treasure never eyesight got, nor was ever guessed what for
>   the hearing?

27

No, but it was not these.
The jading and jar of the cart,
Time's tasking, it is fathers that asking for ease
'Of the sodden-with-its-sorrowing heart,
Not danger, electrical horror; then further it finds
The appealing of the Passion is tenderer in prayer apart:
Other, I gather, in measure her mind's
Burden, in wind's burly and beat of endragonèd seas.

28

But how shall I . . . make me room there:
Reach me a . . . Fancy, come faster—
Strike you the sight of it? look at it loom there,
Thing that she . . . there then! the Master,
Ipse, the only one, Christ, King, Head:
He was to cure the extremity where he had cast her;
Do, deal, lord it with living and dead;
Let him ride, her pride, in his triumph, despatch and have done
    with his doom there.

29

Ah! there was a heart right!
There was single eye!
Read the unshapeable shock night
And knew the who and the why;
Wording it how but by him that present and past,
Heaven and earth are word of, worded by?—
The Simon Peter of a soul! to the blast
Tarpeian-fast, but a blown beacon of light.

30

Jesu, heart's light,
Jesu, maid's son,
What was the feast followed the night
Thou hadst glory of this nun?—

Feast of the one woman without stain.
For so conceivèd, so to conceive thee is done;
    But here was heart-throe, birth of a brain,
Word, that heard and kept thee and uttered thee outright.

31

        Well, she has thee for the pain, for the
        Patience; but pity of the rest of them!
    Heart, go and bleed at a bitterer vein for the
        Comfortless unconfessed of them—
No not uncomforted: lovely-felicitous Providence
Finger of a tender of, O of a feathery delicacy, the breast of the
        Maiden could obey so, be a bell to, ring of it, and
Startle the poor sheep back! is the shipwrack then a harvest,
    does tempest carry the grain for thee?

32

        I admire thee, master of the tides,
        Of the Yore-flood, of the year's fall;
    The recurb and the recovery of the gulf's sides,
        The girth of it and the wharf of it and the wall;
Stanching, quenching ocean of a motionable mind;
Ground of being, and granite of it: past all
        Grasp God, throned behind
Death with a sovereignty that heeds but hides, bodes but abides;

33

        With a mercy that outrides
        The all of water, an ark
    For the listener; for the lingerer with a love glides
        Lower than death and the dark;
A vein for the visiting of the past-prayer, pent in prison,
The-last-breath penitent spirits—the uttermost mark
        Our passion-plungèd giant risen,
The Christ of the Father compassionate, fetched in the storm
    of his strides.

34

Now burn, new born to the world,
    Double-naturèd name,
The heaven-flung, heart-fleshed, maiden-furled
    Miracle-in-Mary-of-flame,
Mid-numberèd He in three of the thunder-throne!
Not a dooms-day dazzle in his coming nor dark as he
    came;
    Kind, but royally reclaiming his own;
A released shower, let flash to the shire, not a lightning of fire
    hard-hurled.

35

    Dame, at our door
    Drowned, and among our shoals,
Remember us in the roads, the heaven-haven of the
    Reward:
    Our King back, oh, upon English souls!
Let him easter in us, be a dayspring to the dimness of us,
    be a crimson-cresseted east,
More brightening her, rare-dear Britain, as his reign rolls,
    Pride, rose, prince, hero of us, high-priest,
Our hearts' charity's hearth's fire, our thoughts' chivalry's
    throng's Lord.

MOONRISE

I awoke in the Midsummer not to call night, | in the white
    and the walk of the morning:
The moon, dwindled and thinned to the fringe | of a finger-nail
    held to the candle,
Or paring of paradisaïcal fruit, | lovely in waning but lustre-
    less,
Stepped from the stool, drew back from the barrow, | of dark
    Maenefa the mountain;

A cusp still clasped him, a fluke yet fanged him, | entangled   5
　　him, not quit utterly.
This was the prized, the desirable sight, | unsought, presented
　　so easily,
Parted me leaf and leaf, divided me, | eyelid and eyelid of
　　slumber.

THE SILVER JUBILEE:

*To James First Bishop of Shrewsbury on the
25th Year of his Episcopate July 28. 1876*

　·Though no high-hung bells or din
　Of braggart bugles cry it in—
　　　What is sound? Nature's round
　Makes the Silver Jubilee.

　Five and twenty years have run   5
　Since sacred fountains to the sun
　　　Sprang, that but now were shut,
　Showering Silver Jubilee.

　Feasts, when we shall fall asleep,
　Shrewsbury may see others keep;   10
　　　None but you this her true,
　This her Silver Jubilee.

　Not today we need lament
　Your wealth of life is some way spent:
　　　Toil has shed round your head   15
　Silver but for Jubilee.

　Then for her whose velvet vales
　Should have pealed with welcome, Wales,
　　　Let the chime of a rhyme
　Utter Silver Jubilee.   20

PENMAEN POOL

For the Visitors' Book at the Inn

Who long for rest, who look for pleasure
Away from counter, court, or school
O where live well your lease of leisure
But here at, here at Penmaen Pool?

You'll dare the Alp? you'll dart the skiff?—   5
Each sport has here its tackle and tool:
Come, plant the staff by Cadair cliff;
Come, swing the sculls on Penmaen Pool.

What's yonder?—Grizzled Dyphwys dim:
The triple-hummocked Giant's stool,   10
Hoar messmate, hobs and nobs with him
To halve the bowl of Penmaen Pool.

And all the landscape under survey,
At tranquil turns, by nature's rule,
Rides repeated topsyturvy   15
In frank, in fairy Penmaen Pool.

And Charles's Wain, the wondrous seven,
And sheep-flock clouds like worlds of wool,
For all they shine so, high in heaven,
Shew brighter shaken in Penmaen Pool.   20

The Mawddach, how she trips! though throttled
If floodtide teeming thrills her full,
And mazy sands all water-wattled
Waylay her at ebb, past Penmaen Pool.

But what's to see in stormy weather,   25
When grey showers gather and gusts are cool?—
Why, raindrop-roundels looped together
That lace the face of Penmaen Pool.

Then even in weariest wintry hour
Of New Year's month or surly Yule   30
Furred snows, charged tuft above tuft, tower
From darksome darksome Penmaen Pool.

And ever, if bound here hardest home,
You've parlour-pastime left and (who'll
Not honour it?) ale like goldy foam   35
That frocks an oar in Penmaen Pool.

Then come who pine for peace or pleasure
Away from counter, court, or school,
Spend here your measure of time and treasure
And taste the treats of Penmaen Pool.   40

GOD'S GRANDEUR

The world is charged with the grandeur of God.
  It will flame out, like shining from shook foil;
  It gathers to a greatness, like the ooze of oil
Crushed. Why do men then now not reck his rod?
Generations have trod, have trod, have trod;   5
  And all is seared with trade; bleared, smeared with toil;
  And wears man's smudge and shares man's smell: the soil
Is bare now, nor can foot feel, being shod.

And for all this, nature is never spent;
  There lives the dearest freshness deep down things;   10
And though the last lights off the black West went
  Oh, morning, at the brown brink eastward, springs—
Because the Holy Ghost over the bent
  World broods with warm breast and with ah! bright wings.

THE STARLIGHT NIGHT

Look at the stars! look, look up at the skies!
  O look at all the fire-folk sitting in the air!
  The bright boroughs, the circle-citadels there!
Down in dim woods the diamond delves! the elves'-eyes!
The grey lawns cold where gold, where quickgold lies!   5
  Wind-beat whitebeam! airy abeles set on a flare!
  Flake-doves sent floating forth at a farmyard scare!—
Ah well! it is all a purchase, all is a prize.

Buy then! bid then!—What?—Prayer, patience, alms, vows.
Look, look: a May-mess, like on orchard boughs!   10
  Look! March-bloom, like on mealed-with-yellow sallows!
These are indeed the barn; withindoors house
The shocks. This piece-bright paling shuts the spouse
  Christ home, Christ and his mother and all his hallows.

SPRING

Nothing is so beautiful as spring—
  When weeds, in wheels, shoot long and lovely and lush;
  Thrush's eggs look little low heavens, and thrush
Through the echoing timber does so rinse and wring
The ear, it strikes like lightnings to hear him sing;   5
  The glassy peartree leaves and blooms, they brush
  The descending blue; that blue is all in a rush
With richness; the racing lambs too have fair their fling.

What is all this juice and all this joy?
  A strain of the earth's sweet being in the beginning   10
In Eden garden.—Have, get, before it cloy,
  Before it cloud, Christ, lord, and sour with sinning,
Innocent mind and Mayday in girl and boy,
  Most, O maid's child, thy choice and worthy the winning.

IN THE VALLEY OF THE ELWY

I remember a house where all were good
  To me, God knows, deserving no such thing:
  Comforting smell breathed at very entering,
Fetched fresh, as I suppose, off some sweet wood.
That cordial air made those kind people a hood   5
    All over, as a bevy of eggs the mothering wing
    Will, or mild nights the new morsels of spring:
Why, it seemed of course; seemed of right it should.

Lovely the woods, waters, meadows, combes, vales,
All the air things wear that build this world of Wales;   *10*
  Only the inmate does not correspond:
God, lover of souls, swaying considerate scales,
Complete thy creature dear O where it fails,
  Being mighty a master, being a father and fond.

THE SEA AND THE SKYLARK

On ear and ear two noises too old to end
  Trench—right, the tide that ramps against the shore;
  With a flood or a fall, low lull-off or all roar,
Frequenting there while moon shall wear and wend.

Left hand, off land, I hear the lark ascend,   5
  His rash-fresh re-winded new-skeinèd score
  In crisps of curl off wild winch whirl, and pour
And pelt music, till none's to spill nor spend.

How these two shame this shallow and frail town!
  How ring right out our sordid turbid time,   *10*
Being pure! We, life's pride and cared-for crown,

Have lost that cheer and charm of earth's past prime:
Our make and making break, are breaking, down
   To man's last dust, drain fast towards man's first slime.

THE WINDHOVER:

To Christ our Lord

I caught this morning morning's minion, king-
   dom of daylight's dauphin, dapple-dawn-drawn Falcon, in
         his riding
Of the rolling level underneath him steady air, and striding
High there, how he rung upon the rein of a wimpling wing
In his ecstasy! then off, off forth on swing,   5
   As a skate's heel sweeps smooth on a bow-bend: the hurl and
         gliding
   Rebuffed the big wind. My heart in hiding
Stirred for a bird,—the achieve of, the mastery of the thing!

Brute beauty and valour and act, oh, air, pride, plume, here
   Buckle! AND the fire that breaks from thee then, a billion 10
Times told lovelier, more dangerous, O my chevalier!

   No wonder of it: shéer plód makes plough down sillion
Shine, and blue-bleak embers, ah my dear,
   Fall, gall themselves, and gash gold-vermilion.

PIED BEAUTY

Glory be to God for dappled things—
   For skies of couple-colour as a brinded cow;
     For rose-moles all in stipple upon trout that swim;
Fresh-firecoal chestnut-falls; finches' wings;
   Landscape plotted and pieced—fold, fallow, and plough;   5
   And áll trádes, their gear and tackle and trim.

All things counter, original, spare, strange;
   Whatever is fickle, freckled (who knows how?)
     With swift, slow; sweet, sour; adazzle, dim;
He fathers-forth whose beauty is past change: 10
                   Praise him.

HURRAHING IN HARVEST

Summer ends now; now, barbarous in beauty, the stooks rise
   Around; up above, what wind-walks! what lovely
     behaviour
   Of silk-sack clouds! has wilder, wilful-wavier
Meal-drift moulded ever and melted across skies?

I walk, I lift up, I lift up heart, eyes,   5
   Down all that glory in the heavens to glean our Saviour;
   And, éyes, heárt, what looks, what lips yet gave you a
Rapturous love's greeting of realer, of rounder replies?

And the azurous hung hills are his world-wielding shoulder
   Majestic—as a stallion stalwart, very-violet-sweet!—   10
These things, these things were here and but the beholder
   Wanting; which two when they once meet,
The heart rears wings bold and bolder
   And hurls for him, O half hurls earth for him off under his
     feet.

THE CAGED SKYLARK

As a dare-gale skylark scanted in a dull cage
  Man's mounting spirit in his bone-house, mean house,
    dwells—
  That bird beyond the remembering his free fells;
This in drudgery, day-labouring-out life's age.

Though aloft on turf or perch or poor low stage,   5
  Both sing sometímes the sweetest, sweetest spells,
  Yet both droop deadly sómetimes in their cells
Or wring their barriers in bursts of fear or rage.

Not that the sweet-fowl, song-fowl, needs no rest—
Why, hear him, hear him babble and drop down to his nest, *10*
  But his own nest, wild nest, no prison.

Man's spirit will be flesh-bound when found at best,
But uncumbered: meadow-down is not distressed
  For a rainbow footing it nor he for his bónes rísen.

THE LANTERN OUT OF DOORS

Sometimes a lantern moves along the night,
  That interests our eyes. And who goes there?
  I think; where from and bound, I wonder, where,
With, all down darkness wide, his wading light?

Men go by me whom either beauty bright   5
  In mould or mind or what not else makes rare:
  They rain against our much-thick and marsh air
Rich beams, till death or distance buys them quite.

Death or distance soon consumes them: wind
  What most I may eye after, be in at the end   10
I cannot, and out of sight is out of mind.

Christ minds: Christ's interest, what to avow or amend
  There, éyes them, heart wánts, care haúnts, foot fóllows kínd,
Their ránsom, théir rescue, ánd first, fást, last friénd.

THE LOSS OF THE EURYDICE

Foundered March 24. 1878

The Eurydice—it concerned thee, O Lord:
Three hundred souls, O alas! on board,
  Some asleep unawakened, all un-
warned, eleven fathoms fallen

Where she foundered! One stroke   5
Felled and furled them, the hearts of oak!
  And flockbells off the aerial
Downs' forefalls beat to the burial.

For did she pride her, freighted fully, on
Bounden bales or a hoard of bullion?—   10
  Precious passing measure,
Lads and men her lade and treasure.

She had come from a cruise, training seamen—
Men, boldboys soon to be men:
  Must it, worst weather,
Blast bole and bloom together?   15

No Atlantic squall overwrought her
Or rearing billow of the Biscay water:
   Home was hard at hand
And the blow bore from land.   *20*

And you were a liar, O blue March day.
Bright sun lanced fire in the heavenly bay;
   But what black Boreas wrecked her? he
Came equipped, deadly-electric,

A beetling baldbright cloud thorough England   *25*
Riding: there did storms not mingle? and
   Hailropes hustle and grind their
Heavengravel? wolfsnow, worlds of it, wind there?

Now Carisbrook keep goes under in gloom;
Now it overvaults Appledurcombe;   *30*
   Now near by Ventnor town
It hurls, hurls off Boniface Down.

Too proud, too proud, what a press she bore!
Royal, and all her royals wore.
   Sharp with her, shorten sail!   *35*
Too late; lost; gone with the gale.

This was that fell capsize.
As half she had righted and hoped to rise
   Death teeming in by her portholes
Raced down decks, round messes of mortals.   *40*

Then a lurch forward, frigate and men;
'All hands for themselves' the cry ran then;
   But she who had housed them thither
Was around them, bound them or wound them with her.

Marcus Hare, high her captain,   45
Kept to her—care-drowned and wrapped in
    Cheer's death, would follow
His charge through the champ-white water-in-a-wallow,

All under Channel to bury in a beach her
Cheeks: Right, rude of feature,   50
    He thought he heard say
'Her commander! and thou too, and thou this way.'

It is even seen, time's something server,
In mankind's medley a duty-swerver,
    At downright 'No or yes?'   55
Doffs all, drives full for righteousness.

Sydney Fletcher, Bristol-bred,
(Low lie his mates now on watery bed)
    Takes to the seas and snows
As sheer down the ship goes.   60

Now her afterdraught gullies him too down;
Now he wrings for breath with the deathgush brown;
    Till a lifebelt and God's will
Lend him a lift from the sea-swill.

Now he shoots short up to the round air;   65
Now he gasps, now he gazes everywhere;
    But his eye no cliff, no coast or
Mark makes in the rivelling snowstorm.

Him, after an hour of wintry waves,
A schooner sights, with another, and saves,   70
    And he boards her in Oh! such joy
He has lost count what came next, poor boy.—

They say who saw one sea-corpse cold
He was all of lovely manly mould,
   Every inch a tar,   *75*
Of the best we boast our sailors are.

Look, foot to forelock, how all things suit! he
Is strung by duty, is strained to beauty,
   And brown-as-dawning-skinned
With brine and shine and whirling wind.   *80*

O his nimble finger, his gnarled grip!
Leagues, leagues of seamanship
   Slumber in these forsaken
Bones, this sinew, and will not waken.

He was but one like thousands more.   *85*
Day and night I deplore
   My people and born own nation,
Fast foundering own generation.

I might let bygones be—our curse
Of ruinous shrine no hand or, worse,   *90*
   Robbery's hand is busy to
Dress, hoar-hallowèd shrines unvisited;

Only the breathing temple and fleet
Life, this wildworth blown so sweet,
   These daredeaths, ay this crew, in   *95*
Unchrist, all rolled in ruin—

Deeply surely I need to deplore it,
Wondering why my master bore it,
   The riving off that race
So at home, time was, to his truth and grace   *100*

That a starlight-wender of ours would say
The marvellous Milk was Walsingham Way
   And one—but let be, let be:
More, more than was will yet be.—

O well wept, mother have lost son;   *105*
Wept, wife; wept, sweetheart would be one:
   Though grief yield them no good
Yet shed what tears sad truelove should.

But to Christ lord of thunder
Crouch; lay knee by earth low under: *110*
   'Holiest, loveliest, bravest,
Save my hero, O Hero savest.

And the prayer thou hearst me making
Have, at the awful overtaking,
   Heard; have heard and granted   *115*
Grace that day grace was wanted.'

Not that hell knows redeeming,
But for souls sunk in seeming
   Fresh, till doomfire burn all,
Prayer shall fetch pity eternal.   *120*

THE MAY MAGNIFICAT

May is Mary's month, and I
Muse at that and wonder why:
   Her feasts follow reason,
   Dated due to season—

Candlemas, Lady Day;   5
But the Lady Month, May,
    Why fasten that upon her,
    With a feasting in her honour?

Is it only its being brighter
Than the most are must delight her?   10
    Is it opportunest
    And flowers finds soonest?

Ask of her, the mighty mother:
Her reply puts this other
    Question: What is Spring?—   15
    Growth in every thing—

Flesh and fleece, fur and feather,
Grass and greenworld all together;
    Star-eyed strawberry-breasted
    Throstle above her nested   20

Cluster of bugle blue eggs thin
Forms and warms the life within;
    And bird and blossom swell
    In sod or sheath or shell.

All things rising, all things sizing   25
Mary sees, sympathising
    With that world of good,
    Nature's motherhood.

Their magnifying of each its kind
With delight calls to mind   30
    How she did in her stored
    Magnify the Lord.

Well but there was more than this:
Spring's universal bliss
    Much, had much to say   35
    To offering Mary May.

When drop-of-blood-and-foam-dapple
Bloom lights the orchard-apple
    And thicket and thorp are merry
    With silver-surfèd cherry   40

And azuring-over greybell makes
Wood banks and brakes wash wet like lakes
    And magic cuckoocall
    Caps, clears, and clinches all—

This ecstasy all through mothering earth   45
Tells Mary her mirth till Christ's birth
    To remember and exultation
    In God who was her salvation.

BINSEY POPLARS

felled 1879

My aspens dear, whose airy cages quelled,
Quelled or quenched in leaves the leaping sun,
All felled, felled, are all felled;
    Of a fresh and following folded rank
        Not spared, not one   5
        That dandled a sandalled
    Shadow that swam or sank
On meadow and river and wind-wandering
    weed-winding bank.

O if we but knew what we do
　　　　When we delve or hew—　　　　　　　10
　Hack and rack the growing green!
　　　　Since country is so tender
　To touch, her being só slender,
　That, like this sleek and seeing ball
　But a prick will make no eye at all,　　　　15
　Where we, even where we mean
　　　　　　To mend her we end her,
　　　　When we hew or delve:
After-comers cannot guess the beauty been.
　Ten or twelve, only ten or twelve　　　　20
　　　　Strokes of havoc únselve
　　　　　The sweet especial scene,
　Rural scene, a rural scene,
　Sweet especial rural scene.

DUNS SCOTUS'S OXFORD

Towery city and branchy between towers;
Cuckoo-echoing, bell-swarmèd, lark-charmèd, rook-racked,
　　river-rounded;
The dapple-eared lily below thee; that country and town did
Once encounter in, here coped and poisèd powers;

Thou hast a base and brickish skirt there, sours　　　　5
That neighbour-nature thy grey beauty is grounded
Best in; graceless growth, thou hast confounded
Rural rural keeping—folk, flocks, and flowers.

Yet ah! this air I gather and I release
He lived on; these weeds and waters, these walls are what　10
He haunted who of all men most sways my spirits to peace;

Of realty the rarest-veinèd unraveller; a not
Rivalled insight, be rival Italy or Greece;
Who fired France for Mary without spot.

HENRY PURCELL

The poet wishes well to the divine genius of Purcell and praises him that, whereas other musicians have given utterance to the moods of man's mind, he has, beyond that, uttered in notes the very make and species of man as created both in him and in all men generally.

Have fair fallen, O fair, fair have fallen, so dear
To me, so arch-especial a spirit as heaves in Henry Purcell,
An age is now since passed, since parted; with the reversal
Of the outward sentence low lays him, listed to a heresy, here.

Not mood in him nor meaning, proud fire or sacred fear,   5
Or love or pity or all that sweet notes not his might nursle:
It is the forgèd feature finds me; it is the rehearsal
Of own, of abrúpt sélf there so thrusts on, so throngs the ear.

Let him Oh! with his air of angels then lift me, lay me! only I'll
Have an eye to the sakes of him, quaint moonmarks, to his
        pelted plumage under   10
Wings: so some great stormfowl, whenever he has walked his
        while

The thunder-purple seabeach plumèd purple-of-thunder,
If a wuthering of his palmy snow-pinions scatter a colossal
        smile
Off him, but meaning motion fans fresh our wits with wonder.

THE CANDLE INDOORS

Some candle clear burns somewhere I come by.
I muse at how its being puts blissful back
With yellowy moisture mild night's blear-all black,
Or to-fro tender trambeams truckle at the eye.
By that window what task what fingers ply,   5
I plod wondering, a-wanting, just for lack
Of answer the eagerer a-wanting Jessy or Jack
There God to aggrándise, God to glorify.—

Come you indoors, come home; your fading fire
Mend first and vital candle in close heart's vault: 10
You there are master, do your own desire;
What hinders? Are you beam-blind, yet to a fault
In a neighbour deft-handed? Are you that liar
And, cast by conscience out, spendsavour salt?

THE HANDSOME HEART:

at a Gracious Answer

'But tell me, child, your choice; what shall I buy
You?'—'Father, what you buy me I like best.'
With the sweetest air that said, still plied and pressed,
He swung to his first poised purport of reply.

What the heart is! which, like carriers let fly—   5
Doff darkness, homing nature knows the rest—
To its own fine function, wild and self-instressed,
Falls light as ten years long taught how to and why.

Mannerly-hearted! more than handsome face—
Beauty's bearing or muse of mounting vein,   10
All, in this case, bathed in high hallowing grace . . .

Of heaven what boon to buy you, boy, or gain
Not granted!—Only . . . O on that path you pace
Run all your race, O brace sterner that strain!

THE BUGLER'S FIRST COMMUNION

A bugler boy from barrack (it is over the hill
There)—boy bugler, born, he tells me, of Irish
   Mother to an English sire (he
Shares their best gifts surely, fall how things will),

This very very day came down to us after a boon he on   5
My late being there begged of me, overflowing
   Boon in my bestowing,
Came, I say, this day to it—to a First Communion.

Here he knelt then ín regimental red.
Forth Christ from cupboard fetched, how fain I of feet 10
   To his youngster take his treat!
Low-latched in leaf-light housel his too huge godhead.

There! and your sweetest sendings, ah divine,
By it, heavens, befall him! as a heart Christ's darling, dauntless;
   Tongue true, vaunt- and tauntless; 15
Breathing bloom of a chastity in mansex fine.

Frowning and forefending angel-warder
Squander the hell-rook ranks sally to molest him;
   March, kind comrade, abreast him;
Dress his days to a dexterous and starlight order. 20

How it dóes my heart good, visiting at that bleak hill,
When limber liquid youth, that to all I teach
        Yields tender as a pushed peach,
Hies headstrong to its wellbeing of a self-wise self-will!

Then though I should tread tufts of consolation   25
Dáys áfter, só I in a sort deserve to
        And do serve God to serve to
Just such slips of soldiery Christ's royal ration.

Nothing élse is like it, no, not all so strains
Us: fresh youth fretted in a bloomfall all portending   30
        That sweet's sweeter ending;
Realm both Christ is heir to and thére réigns.

O now well work that sealing sacred ointment!
O for now charms, arms, what bans off bad
        And locks love ever in a lad!   35
Let mé though see no more of him, and not disappointment

Those sweet hopes quell whose least me quickenings lift,
In scarlet or somewhere of some day seeing
        That brow and bead of being,
An our day's God's own Galahad. Though this child's drift 40

Seems by a divíne doom chánnelled, nor do I cry
Disaster there; but may he not rankle and roam
        In backwheels though bound home?—
That left to the Lord of the Eucharist, I here lie by;

Recorded only, I have put my lips on pleas   45
Would brandle adamantine heaven with ride and jar, did
        Prayer go disregarded:
Forward-like, but however, and like favourable heaven heard
   these.

MORNING MIDDAY AND EVENING SACRIFICE

The dappled die-away
Cheek and wimpled lip,
The gold-wisp, the airy-grey
Eye, all in fellowship—
This, all this beauty blooming,   5
This, all this freshness fuming,
Give God while worth consuming.

Both thought and thew now bolder
And told by Nature: Tower;
Head, heart, hand, heel, and shoulder   10
That beat and breathe in power—
This pride of prime's enjoyment
Take as for tool, not toy meant
And hold at Christ's employment.

The vault and scope and schooling   15
And mastery in the mind,
In silk-ash kept from cooling,
And ripest under rind—
What life half lifts the latch of,
What hell stalks towards the snatch of,   20
Your offering, with despatch, of!

ANDROMEDA

Now Time's Andromeda on this rock rude,
With not her either beauty's equal or
Her injury's, looks off by both horns of shore,
Her flower, her piece of being, doomed dragon's food.
        Time past she has been attempted and pursued   5
By many blows and banes; but now hears roar
A wilder beast from West than all were, more
Rife in her wrongs, more lawless, and more lewd.

Her Perseus linger and leave her tó her extremes?—
Pillowy air he treads a time and hangs   10
His thoughts on her, foresaken that she seems,
    All while her patience, morselled into pangs,
Mounts, then to alight disarming, no one dreams,
With Gorgon's gear and barebill, thongs and fangs.

PEACE

When will you ever, Peace, wild wooddove, shy wings shut,
Your round me roaming end, and under be my boughs?
When, when, Peace, will you, Peace? I'll not play hypocrite
To own my heart: I yield you do come sometimes; but
That piecemeal peace is poor peace. What pure peace allows   5
Alarms of wars, the daunting wars, the death of it?

O surely, reaving Peace, my Lord leave in lieu
Some good! And so he does leave Patience exquisite,
That plumes to Peace thereafter. And when Peace here does
    house
He comes with work to do, he does not come to coo,   10
              He comes to brood and sit.

AT THE WEDDING MARCH

    God with honour hang your head,
    Groom, and grace you, bride, your bed
    With lissome scions, sweet scions,
    Out of hallowed bodies bred.

    Each be other's comfort kind: 5
    Déep, déeper than divined,
    Divine charity, dear charity,
    Fast you ever, fast bind.

Then let the March tread our ears:
I to him turn with tears   *10*
Who to wedlock, his wonder wedlock,
Déals tríumph and immortal years.

FELIX RANDAL

Felix Randal the farrier, O is he dead then? my duty all
    ended,
Who have watched his mould of man, big-boned and hardy-
    handsome
Pining, pining, till time when reason rambled in it and some
Fatal four disorders, fleshed there, all contended?

Sickness broke him. Impatient he cursed at first, but mended *5*
Being anointed and all; though a heavenlier heart began some
Months earlier, since I had our sweet reprieve and ransom
Tendered to him. Ah well, God rest him all road ever he
    offended!

This seeing the sick endears them to us, us too it endears.
My tongue had taught thee comfort, touch had quenched thy
    tears,   *10*
Thy tears that touched my heart, child, Felix, poor Felix
    Randal;

How far from then forethought of, all thy more boisterous
    years,
When thou at the random grim forge, powerful admidst peers,
Didst fettle for the great grey drayhorse his bright and battering
    sandal!

BROTHERS

How lovely the elder brother's
Life all laced in the other's,
Lóved-laced!—what once I well
Witnessed; so fortune fell.
When Shrovetide, two years gone,   5
Our boys' plays brought on
Part was picked for John,
Young Jóhn: then fear, then joy
Ran revel in the elder boy.
Their night was come now; all   10
Our company thronged the hall;
Henry, by the wall,
Beckoned me beside him:
I came where called, and eyed him
By meanwhiles; making mý play   15
Turn most on tender byplay.
For, wrung all on love's rack,
My lad, and lost in Jack,
Smiled, blushed, and bit his lip;
Or drove, with a diver's dip,   20
Clutched hands down through clasped knees—
Truth's tokens tricks like these,
Old telltales, with what stress
He hung on the imp's success.
Now the other was bráss-bóld: 25
Hé had no work to hold
His heart up at the strain;
Nay, roguish ran the vein.
Two tedious acts were past;
Jack's call and cue at last;   30
When Henry, heart-forsook,
Dropped eyes and dared not look.
Eh, how áll rúng!
Young dog, he did give tongue!
But Harry—in his hands he has flung   35

His tear-tricked cheeks of flame
For fond love and for shame.
    Ah Nature, framed in fault,
There's comfort then, there's salt;
Nature, bad, base, and blind,   *40*
Dearly thou canst be kind;
There dearly thén, deárly,
I'll cry thou canst be kind.

SPRING AND FALL:

to a young child

Márgarét, áre you gríeving
Over Goldengrove unleaving?
Leáves, líke the things of man, you
With your fresh thoughts care for, can you?
Áh! ás the heart grows older   *5*
It will come to such sights colder
By and by, nor spare a sigh
Though worlds of wanwood leafmeal lie;
And yet you wíll weep and know why,
Now no matter, child, the name: *10*
Sórrow's spríngs áre the same.
Nor mouth had, no nor mind, expressed
What heart heard of, ghost guessed:
It ís the blight man was born for,
It is Margaret you mourn for.   *15*

INVERSNAID

This darksome burn, horseback brown,
His rollrock highroad roaring down,
In coop and in comb the fleece of his foam
Flutes and low to the lake falls home.

A windpuff-bonnet of fáwn-fróth   5
Turns and twindles over the broth
Of a pool so pitchblack, féll-frówning,
It rounds and rounds Despair to drowning.

Degged with dew, dappled with dew
Are the groins of the braes that the brook treads through, 10
Wiry heathpacks, flitches of fern,
And the beadbonny ash that sits over the burn.

What would the world be, once bereft
Of wet and of wildness? Let them be left,
O let them be left, wildness and wet;   15
Long live the weeds and the wilderness yet.

As kingfishers catch fire, dragonflies dráw fláme;
As tumbled over rim in roundy wells
Stones ring; like each tucked string tells, each hung bell's
Bow swung finds tongue to fling out broad its name;
Each mortal thing does one thing and the same: 5
Deals out that being indoors each one dwells;
Selves—goes itself; *myself* it speaks and spells,
Crying *Whát I do is me: for that I came.*

I say móre: the just man justices;
Kéeps gráce: thát keeps all his goings graces;   *10*
Acts in God's eye what in God's eye he is—
Chríst—for Christ plays in ten thousand places,
Lovely in limbs, and lovely in eyes not his
To the Father through the features of men's faces.

RIBBLESDALE

Earth, sweet Earth, sweet landscape, with leavès throng
And louchèd low grass, heaven that dost appeal
To, with no tongue to plead, no heart to feel;
That canst but only be, but dost that long—

Thou canst but be, but that thou well dost; strong   *5*
Thy plea with him who dealt, nay does now deal,
Thy lovely dale down thus and thus bids reel
Thy river, and o'er gives all to rack or wrong.

    And what is Earth's eye, tongue, or heart else, where
Else, but in dear and dogged man?—Ah, the heir   *10*
To his own selfbent so bound, so tied to his turn,
To thriftless reave both our rich round world bare
And none reck of world after, this bids wear
Earth brows of such care, care and dear concern.

THE LEADEN ECHO AND THE GOLDEN ECHO

(Maidens' song from St. Winefred's Well)

THE LEADEN ECHO

How to kéep—is there ány any, is there none such, nowhere
    known some, bow or brooch or braid or brace, láce,
    latch or catch or key to keep
Back beauty, keep it, beauty, beauty, beauty, . . . from vanish-
    ing away?
Ó is there no frowning of these wrinkles, rankèd wrinkles
    deep,
Dówn? no waving off of these most mournful messengers,
    still messengers, sad and stealing messengers of grey?
No there's none, there's none, O no there's none,   5
Nor can you long be, what you now are, called fair,
Do what you may do, what, do what you may,
And wisdom is early to despair:
Be beginning; since, no, nothing can be done
To keep at bay   10
Age and age's evils, hoar hair,
Ruck and wrinkle, drooping, dying, death's worst, winding
    sheets, tombs and worms and tumbling to decay;
So be beginning, be beginning to despair.
O there's none; no no no there's none:
Be beginning to despair, to despair,   15
Despair, despair, despair, despair.

THE GOLDEN ECHO

        Spare!
There ís one, yes I have one (Hush there!);
Only not within seeing of the sun.
Not within the singeing of the strong sun,   20

Tall sun's tingeing, or treacherous the tainting of the earth's
    air,
Somewhere elsewhere there is ah well where! one,
Óne. Yes I can tell such a key, I do know such a place,
Where whatever's prized and passes of us, everything that's
    fresh and fast flying of us, seems to us sweet of us and
    swifly away with, done away with, undone,
Undone, done with, soon done with, and yet dearly and
    dangerously sweet   25
Of us, the wimpled-water-dimpled, not-by-morning-matchèd
    face,
The flower of beauty, fleece of beauty, too too apt to, ah! to
    fleet,
Never fleets móre, fastened with the tenderest truth
To its own best being and its loveliness of youth: it is an ever-
    lastingness of, O it is an all youth!
Come then, your ways and airs and looks, locks, maiden gear,
    gallantry and gaiety and grace,   30
Winning ways, airs innocent, maiden manners, sweet looks,
    loose locks, long locks, lovelocks, gaygear, going gallant,
    girlgrace—
Resign them, sign them, seal them, send them, motion them
    with breath,
And with sighs soaring, soaring síghs deliver
Them; beauty-in-the-ghost, deliver it, early now, long before
    death
Give beauty back, beauty, beauty, beauty, back to God,
    beauty's self and beauty's giver.   35
See; not a hair is, not an eyelash, not the least lash lost; every
    hair
Is, hair of the head, numbered.
Nay, what we had lighthanded left in surly the mere mould
Will have waked and have waxed and have walked with the
    wind what while we slept,
This side, that side hurling a heavyheaded hundredfold   40
What while we, while we slumbered.
O then, weary then whý should we tread? O why are we so

haggard at the heart, so care-coiled, care-killed, so fagged,
   so fashed, so cogged, so cumbered,
When the thing we freely fórfeit is kept with fonder a care,
Fonder a care kept than we could have kept it, kept
Far with fonder a care (and we, we should have lost it) finer,
   fonder   45
A care kept.—Where kept? do but tell us where kept, where.—
Yonder.—What high as that! We follow, now we follow.—
   Yonder, yes yonder, yonder,
Yonder.

THE BLESSED VIRGIN COMPARED TO THE AIR
WE BREATHE

     Wild air, world-mothering air,
     Nestling me everywhere,
     That each eyelash or hair
     Girdles; goes home betwixt
     The fleeciest, frailest-flixed   5
     Snowflake; that's fairly mixed
     With, riddles, and is rife
     In every least thing's life;
     This needful, never spent,
     And nursing element;   10
     My more than meat and drink,
     My meal at every wink;
     This air, which, by life's law,
     My lung must draw and draw
     Now but to breathe its praise,   15
     Minds me in many ways
     Of her who not only
     Gave God's infinity
     Dwindled to infancy
     Welcome in womb and breast,   20
     Birth, milk, and all the rest

But mothers each new grace
That does now reach our race—
Mary Immaculate,
Merely a woman, yet   25
Whose presence, power is
Great as no goddess's
Was deemèd, dreamèd; who
This one work has to do—
Let all God's glory through,   30
God's glory which would go
Through her and from her flow
Off, and no way but so.

I say that we are wound
With mercy round and round 35
As if with air: the same
Is Mary, more by name.
She, wild web, wondrous robe,
Mantles the guilty globe,
Since God has let dispense   40
Her prayers his providence:
Nay, more than almoner,
The sweet alms' self is her
And men are meant to share
Her life as life does air.   45
If I have understood,
She holds high motherhood
Towards all our ghostly good
And plays in grace her part
About man's beating heart,   50
Laying, like air's fine flood,
The deathdance in his blood;
Yet no part but what will
Be Christ our Saviour still.
Of her flesh he took flesh:
He does take fresh and fresh, 55
Though much the mystery how,

Not flesh but spirit now
And makes, O marvellous!
New Nazareths in us,   60
Where she shall yet conceive
Him, morning, noon, and eve;
New Bethlems, and he born
There, evening, noon, and morn—
Bethlem or Nazareth,   65
Men here may draw like breath
More Christ and baffle death;
Who, born so, comes to be
New self and nobler me
In each one and each one   70
More makes, when all is done,
Both God's and Mary's Son.
    Again, look overhead
How air is azurèd;
O how! nay do but stand   75
Where you can lift your hand
Skywards: rich, rich it laps
Round the four fingergaps.
Yet such a sapphire-shot,
Charged, steepèd sky will not   80
Stain light. Yea, mark you this:
It does no prejudice.
The glass-blue days are those
When every colour glows,
Each shape and shadow shows.   85
Blue be it: this blue heaven
The seven or seven times seven
Hued sunbeam will transmit
Perfect, not alter it.
Or if there does some soft,   90
On things aloof, aloft,
Bloom breathe, that one breath more
Earth is the fairer for.
Whereas did air not make

This bath of blue and slake 95
His fire, the sun would shake,
A blear and blinding ball
With blackness bound, and all
The thick stars round him roll
Flashing like flecks of coal, 100
Quartz-fret, or sparks of salt,
In grimy vasty vault.
    So God was god of old:
A mother came to mould
Those limbs like ours which are 105
What must make our daystar
Much dearer to mankind;
Whose glory bare would blind
Or less would win man's mind.
Through her we may see him 110
Made sweeter, not made dim,
And her hand leaves his light
Sifted to suit our sight.
    Be thou then, O thou dear
Mother, my atmosphere; 115
My happier world, wherein
To wend and meet no sin;
Above me, round me lie
Fronting my froward eye
With sweet and scarless sky; 120
Stir in my ears, speak there
Of God's love, O live air,
Of patience, penance, prayer:
World-mothering air, air wild,
Wound with thee, in thee isled, 125
Fold home, fast fold thy child.

Not of all my eyes see, wandering on the world,
Is anything a milk to the mind so, so sighs deep
Poetry to it, as a tree whose boughs break in the sky.
Say it is ashboughs: whether on a December day and furled
Fast ór they in clammyish lashtender combs creep   5
Apart wide and new-nestle at heaven most high.
They touch heaven, tabour on it; how their talons sweep
The smouldering enormous winter welkin! May
Mells blue and snowwhite through them, a fringe and fray
Of greenery: it is old earth's groping towards the steep   10
          Heaven whom she childs us by.

SPELT FROM SIBYL'S LEAVES

Earnest, earthless, equal, attuneable, | vaulty, voluminous,
       . . . stupendous
Evening strains to be tíme's vást, | womb-of-all, home-of-all,
       hearse-of-all night.
Her fond yellow hornlight wound to the west, | her wild
       hollow hoarlight hung to the height
Waste; her earliest stars, earl-stars, | stárs principal, overbend
       us,
Fíre-féaturing heaven. For earth | her being has unbound; her
       dapple is at an end, as-   5
tray or aswarm, all thoughther, in throngs; | self ín self
       steepèd and páshed—qúite
Disremembering, dísmémbering | áll now. Heart, you round
       me right
With: Óur évening is over us; óur night | whélms, whélms,
       ánd will end us.
Only the beak-leaved boughs dragonish | damask the tool-
       smooth bleak light; black,
Ever so black on it. Óur tale, O óur oracle! | Lét life, wáned,
       ah lét life wind   10

Off hér once skéined stained véined varíety | upon, áll on twó
    spools; párt, pen, páck
Now her áll in twó flocks, twó folds—black, white; | right,
    wrong; reckon but, reck but, mind
But thése two; wáre of a wórld where bút these | twó tell, each
    off the óther; of a rack
Where, selfwrung, selfstrung, sheathe- and shelterless, | thóughts
    agaínst thoughts ín groans grínd.

TO WHAT SERVES MORTAL BEAUTY?

To what serves mortal beauty | —dangerous; does set danc-
ing blood—the O-seal-that-so | feature, flung prouder form
Than Purcell tune lets tread to? | See: it does this: keeps warm
Men's wits to the things that are; | what good means—where a
    glance
Master more may than gaze, | gaze out of countenance.   5
Those lovely lads once, wet-fresh | windfalls of war's storm,
How then should Gregory, a father, | have gleanèd else from
    swarm-
èd Rome? But God to a nation | dealt that day's dear chance.
    To man, that needs would worship| block or barren stone,
Our law says: Love what are | love's worthiest, were all known; 10
World's loveliest—men's selves. Self | flashes off frame and
    face.
What do then? how meet beauty? | Merely meet it; own,
Home at heart, heaven's sweet gift; | then leave, let that alone.
Yea, wish that though, wish all, | God's better beauty, grace.

Yes. Whý do we áll, seeing of a soldier, bless him? bless
Our redcoats, our tars? Both these being, the greater part,
But frail clay, nay but foul clay. Here it is: the heart,
Since, proud, it calls the calling manly, gives a guess
That, hopes that, makesbelieve, the men must be no less;   5
It fancies, feigns, deems, dears the artist after his art;
And fain will find as sterling all as all is smart,
And scarlet wear the spirit of wár thére express.

Mark Christ our King. He knows war, served this soldiering
　　through;
He of all can reeve a rope best. There he bides in bliss   10
Now, and séeing somewhére some mán do all that man can do,
For love he leans forth, needs his neck must fall on, kiss,
And cry 'O Christ-done deed! So God-made-flesh does too:
Were I come o'er again' cries Christ 'it should be this'.

Not, I'll not, carrion comfort, Despair, not feast on thee;
Not untwist —slack they may be—these last strands of man
In me ór, most weary, cry *I can no more*. I can;
Can something, hope, wish day come, not choose not to be.
But ah, but O thou terrible, why wouldst thou rude on me   5
Thy wring-world right foot rock? lay a lionlimb against me?
　　scan
With darksome devouring eyes my bruisèd bones? and fan,
O in turns of tempest, me heaped there; me frantic to avoid
　　thee and flee?

　　Why? That my chaff might fly; my grain lie, sheer and clear.
Nay in all that toil, that coil, since (seems) I kissed the rod,   10
Hand rather, my heart lo! lapped strength, stole joy, would
　　laugh, chéer.

Cheer whom though? The hero whose heaven-handling flung
 me, fóot tród
Me? or me that fought him? O which one? is it each one?
 That night, that year
Of now done darkness I wretch lay wrestling with (my God!)
 my God.

No worst, there is none. Pitched past pitch of grief,
More pangs will, schooled at forepangs, wilder wring.
Comforter, where, where is your comforting?
Mary, mother of us, where is your relief?
My cries heave, herds-long; huddle in a main, a chief- 5
woe, world-sorrow; on an age-old anvil wince and sing—
Then lull, then leave off. Fury had shrieked 'No ling-
ering! Let me be fell: force I must be brief'.

 O the mind, mind has mountains; cliffs of fall
Frightful, sheer, no-man-fathomed. Hold them cheap 10
May who ne'er hung there. Nor does long our small
Durance deal with that steep or deep. Here! creep,
Wretch, under a comfort serves in a whirlwind: all
Life death does end and each day dies with sleep.

To seem the stranger lies my lot, my life
Among strangers. Father and mother dear,
Brothers and sisters are in Christ not near
And he my peace my parting, sword and strife.
 England, whose honour O all my heart woos, wife 5
To my creating thought, would neither hear

Me, were I pleading, plead nor do I: I wear-
y of idle a being but by where wars are rife.

    I am in Ireland now; now I am at a thírd
Remove. Not but in all removes I can   10
Kind love both give and get. Only what word
Wisest my heart breeds dark heaven's baffling ban
Bars or hell's spell thwarts. This to hoard unheard,
Heard unheeded, leaves me a lonely begán.

I wake and feel the fell of dark, not day.
What hours, O what black hoürs we have spent
This night! what sights you, heart, saw; ways you went!
And more must, in yet longer light's delay.
    With witness I speak this. But where I say   5
Hours I mean years, mean life. And my lament
Is cries countless, cries like dead letters sent
To dearest him that lives alas! away.

    I am gall, I am heartburn. God's most deep decree
Bitter would have me taste: my taste was me;   10
Bones built in me, flesh filled, blood brimmed the curse.
    Selfyeast of spirit a dull dough sours. I see
The lost are like this, and their scourge to be
As I am mine, their sweating selves; but worse.

Patience, hard thing! the hard thing but to pray,
But bid for, Patience is! Patience who asks
Wants war, wants wounds; weary his times, his tasks;

To do without, take tosses, and obey.
    Rare patience roots in these, and, these away,   5
Nowhere. Natural heart's ivy, Patience masks
Our ruins of wrecked past purpose. There she basks
Purple eyes and seas of liquid leaves all day.

    We hear our hearts grate on themselves: it kills
To bruise them dearer. Yet the rebellious wills   10
Of us we do bid God bend to him even so.
    And where is he who more and more distills
Delicious kindness?—He is patient. Patience fills
His crisp combs, and that comes those ways we know.

My own heart let me more have pity on; let
Me live to my sad self hereafter kind,
Charitable; not live this tormented mind
With this tormented mind tormenting yet.
    I cast for comfort I can no more get   5
By groping round my comfortless, than blind
Eyes in their dark can day or thirst can find
Thirst's all-in-all in all a world of wet.

Soul, self; come poor Jackself, I do advise
You, jaded, let be; call off thoughts awhile   10
Elsewhere; leave comfort root-room; let joy size
At God knows when to God knows what; whose smile
's not wrung, see you; unforeseen times rather—as skies
Betweenpie mountains—lights a lovely mile.

TOM'S GARLAND:

upon the Unemployed

Tom—garlanded with squat and surly steel
Tom; then Tom's fallowbootfellow piles pick
By him and rips out rockfire homeforth—sturdy Dick;
Tom Heart-at-ease, Tom Navvy: he is all for his meal
Sure, 's bed now. Low be it: lustily he his low lot (feel   5
That ne'er need hunger, Tom; Tom seldom sick,
Seldomer heartsore; that treads through, prickproof, thick
Thousands of thorns, thoughts) swings though. Commonweal
Little I reck ho! lacklevel in, if all had bread:
What! Country is honour enough in all us—lordly head,   10
With heaven's lights high hung round, or, mother-ground
That mammocks, mighty foot. But no way sped,
Nor mind nor mainstrength; gold go garlanded
With, perilous, O nó; nor yet plod safe shod sound;
        Undenizened, beyond bound   15
Of earth's glory, earth's ease, all; no one, nowhere,
In wide the world's weal; rare gold, bold steel, bare
        In both; care, but share care—
This, by Despair, bred Hangdog dull; by Rage,
Manwolf, worse; and their packs infest the age.   20

HARRY PLOUGHMAN

Hard as hurdle arms, with a broth of goldfish flue
Breathed round; the rack of ribs; the scooped flank; lank
Rope-over thigh; knee-nave; and barrelled shank—
        Head and foot, shoulder and shank—
By a grey eye's heed steered well, one crew, fall to;   5
Stand at stress. Each limb's barrowy brawn, his thew
That onewhere curded, onewhere sucked or sank—
        Soared or sank—,

Though as a beechbole firm, finds his, as at a rollcall, rank
And features, in flesh, what deed he each must do—   10
        His sinew-service where do.

He leans to it, Harry bends, look. Back, elbow, and liquid
    waist
In him, all quail to the wallowing o' the plough: 's cheek
    crimsons; curls
Wag or crossbridle, in a wind lifted, windlaced——
        See his wind- lilylocks -laced;   15
Churlsgrace, too, child of Amansstrength, how it hangs or
    hurls
Them—broad in bluff hide his frowning feet lashed! raced
With, along them, cragiron under and cold furls—
        With-a-fountain's shining-shot furls.

THAT NATURE IS A HERACLITEAN FIRE AND
OF THE COMFORT OF THE RESURRECTION

Cloud-puffball, torn tufts, tossed pillows | fláunt forth, then
    chevy on an air-
built thoroughfare: heaven-roysterers, in gay-gangs | they
    throng; they glitter in marches.
Down roughcast, down dazzling whitewash, | wherever an
    elm arches,
Shivelights and shadowtackle in long | lashes lace, lance, and
    pair.
Delightfully the bright wind boisterous | ropes, wrestles, beats
    earth bare
Of yestertempest's creases; | in pool and rut peel parches   5
Squandering ooze to squeezed | dough, crust, dust; stanches,
    starches
Squadroned masks and manmarks | treadmire toil there
Footfretted in it. Million-fuelèd, | nature's bonfire burns on.

But quench her bonniest, dearest | to her, her clearest-selvèd
    spark   *10*
Man, how fast his firedint, | his mark on mind, is gone!
both are in an unfathomable, all is in an enormous dark
Drowned. O pity and indig | nation! Manshape, that shone
Sheer off, disseveral, a star, | death blots black out; nor mark
              Is any of him at all so stark   *15*
But vastness blurs and time | beats level. Enough! the Resur-
    rection.
A heart's-clarion! Away grief's gasping, | joyless days, de-
    jection.
              Across my foundering deck shone
A beacon, an eternal beam. | Flesh fade, and mortal trash
Fall to the residuary worm; | world's wildfire, leave but ash: *20*
              In a flash, at a trumpet crash,
I am all at once what Christ is, | since he was what I am, and
This Jack, joke, poor potsherd, | patch, matchwood, immortal
    diamond,
              Is immortal diamond.

In honour of

ST ALPHONSUS RODRIGUEZ

Laybrother of the Society of Jesus

Honour is flashed off exploit, so we say;
And those strokes once that gashed flesh or galled shield
Should tongue that time now, trumpet now that field,
And, on the fighter, forge his glorious day.
On Christ they do and on the martyr may;   *5*
But be the war within, the brand we wield
Unseen, the heroic breast not outward-steeled,
Earth hears no hurtle then from fiercest fray.

   Yet God (that hews mountain and continent,
Earth, all, out; who, with trickling increment,   10
Veins violets and tall trees makes more and more)
Could crowd career with conquest while there went
Those years and years by of world without event
That in Majorca Alfonso watched the door.

*Justus quidem tu es, Domine, si disputem tecum: verumtamen
justa loquar ad te: Quare via impiorum prosperatur? &c.*

Thou art indeed just, Lord, if I contend
With thee; but, sir, so what I plead is just.
Why do sinners' ways prosper? and why must
Disappointment all I endeavour end?
      Wert thou my enemy, O thou my friend,   5
How wouldst thou worse, I wonder, than thou dost
Defeat, thwart me? Oh, the sots and thralls of lust
Do in spare hours more thrive than I that spend,
Sir, life upon thy cause. See, banks and brakes
Now, leavèd how thick! lacèd they are again   10
With fretty chervil, look, and fresh wind shakes
Them; birds build—but not I build; no, but strain,
Time's eunuch, and not breed one work that wakes.
Mine, O thou lord of life, send my roots rain.

The shepherd's brow, fronting forked lightning, owns
The horror and the havoc and the glory
Of it. Angels fall, they are towers, from heaven—a story
Of just, majestical, and giant groans.
But man—we, scaffold of score brittle bones;   5
Who breathe, from groundlong babyhood to hoary
Age gasp; whose breath is our *memento mori*—

What bass is *our* viol for tragic tones?
He! Hand to mouth he lives, and voids with shame;
And, blazoned in however bold the name,   *10*
Man Jack the man is, just; his mate a hussy.
And I that die these deaths, that feed this flame,
That . . . in smooth spoons spy life's masque mirrored: tame
My tempests there, my fire and fever fussy.

TO R. B.

The fine delight that fathers thought; the strong
Spur, live and lancing like the blowpipe flame,
Breathes once and, quenchèd faster than it came,
Leaves yet the mind a mother of immortal song.
Nine months she then, nay years, nine years she long   5
Within her wears, bears, cares and combs the same:
The widow of an insight lost she lives, with aim
Now known and hand at work now never wrong.
     Sweet fire the sire of muse, my soul needs this;
I want the one rapture of an inspiration.   10
O then if in my lagging lines you miss
The roll, the rise, the carol, the creation,
My winter world, that scarcely breathes that bliss
Now, yields you, with some sighs, our explanation.

Notes

In the detailed line-by-line annotations, all words and phrases quoted from the poems are in italics.

THE WRECK OF THE DEUTSCHLAND (1875) St Beuno's (*p. 51*)
'What refers to myself in the poem is all strictly and literally true and did all occur.' The real structure of the poem is the bringing into relationship of the poet's profound inner experience and a parallel to it in an event in the outer historical world. The unevadable reality of that outer event was horrifyingly brought home in the reports in *The Times* and the *Illustrated London News*, sent to the poet at St Beuno's by his mother:

> One brave sailor, who was safe in the rigging, went down to try and save a child or woman who was drowning on deck. He was secured by a rope to the rigging, but a wave dashed him against the bulwarks, and when daylight dawned his headless body, detained by the rope, was swaying to and fro with the waves.
>
> (*The Times*, 11 December 1875. cf. stanza 16)

It was in fact with the narrative of the wreck itself that Hopkins started writing the poem (at stanza 12). But he insisted that 'The principal business is lyrical': the work is ultimately an ode rather than a narrative poem. In celebrating and exploring the event, rather than simply recording it, the problem faced was of finding significance in that which appeared merely 'unshapeable' (stanza 29) and cruel, while rejecting any simple notion that the wreck was directly *caused* by God (stanza 6). That significance lay for Hopkins in recognizing the co-presence of terror and beauty in any religious experience of the world: a duality made inevitable since the Fall but made meaningful since the Incarnation and God's own participation in a world of pain. The acceptance of that fact is what is recorded in 'Part the First'; and the literalness of what is described there (see stanza 2) is attested by a private Journal entry of 18 September 1873 describing

> a nervous collapse of the same sort as when one is very tired and holding oneself at stress not to sleep yet/suddenly goes slack and seems to fall and wakes, only on a greater scale and with a loss of muscular control reaching more or less deep; this one to the chest and not further, so that I could speak, whispering at first, then louder . . . I had lost all muscular stress elsewhere but not sensitive, feeling where each limb lay and thinking that I could recover myself if I could move my finger, I said, and the arm and so the whole body. The feeling is terrible: the body no longer swayed as a piece by the nervous and muscular instress seems to fall in and hang like a dead weight on the chest.

From the very first stanza, Hopkins sees the wreck as presenting a renewed challenge to an intellectual ability to accept that kind of experience: 'And after it almost unmade, what with dread,/Thy doing: and dost thou touch me afresh?/Over again I feel thy finger and find thee'. It is this fact of a public event coming home to personal experience that causes the whole poem to pivot on the interpretation (in stanzas 19–30) of the nun's invocation of Christ at the height of the suffering aboard the *Deutschland*. As Hopkins sees it, the nun's sense of Christ's presence *in* the suffering is equivalent to His rebirth in time (stanza 30). It is in this way that the wreck is ultimately seen (stanzas 34–35) as potentially a sign for Britain: 'Dame, *at our door*/ Drowned'.

PART THE FIRST

Stanza 1

1. MASTERING ME: a composite adjective, describing God.
6. ALMOST UNMADE: bouts of spiritual crisis involved for Hopkins a sense of physical disintegration.
6. WHAT WITH DREAD: 'with what dread'.
8. OVER AGAIN: once again (in the event of the shipwreck) Hopkins recognizes God's terrible working, and remembers – next two stanzas – its earlier manifestation in his own personal life.

Stanza 2

1. I DID SAY YES: the paradox of responding positively to, and accepting, the terror of the experience.
5. THOU KNOWEST etc.: i.e. the details of that actual former experience.
8. THE MIDRIFF ASTRAIN etc.: straining with the pressure (*leaning*) of the *stress*, and pierced (*laced*) with its fire.

Stanza 3

3. WHERE WAS A PLACE?: i.e. of peace and refuge.
4. WINGS THAT SPELL: i.e. words of prayer as a means of escape.
5. HEART OF THE HOST: the *host* is the consecrated bread of the Eucharist (Latin 'hostia' – victim).
7. CARRIER-WITTED: the poet's heart has the right homing instinct; the image of a carrier-pigeon.
8. FROM THE FLAME TO THE FLAME etc.: God is in what is fled from, as much as in what is fled to; his *grace* is implicit even in the terror.

Stanza 4

1–4. I AM SOFT SIFT etc.: the image is of sand (*soft sift*) in the top part of the hourglass – appearing unmoved at the sides (*at the wall*/*Fast*), but under-*mined* and sifting downwards in the middle.
6–8. BUT ROPED WITH etc.: the above image of inner disintegration is

replaced by an image of poise and balance. The steady surface of the well, however, is supported by (*roped with*) the hillside rivulets which feed it. This symbolizes the effect of grace – an aspect (*vein*) and revelation (*pressure*) of the promise (*proffer*) of the gospel.

Stanza 5

3. WAFTING HIM OUT OF IT: *him* = Christ.

4. GLORY IN THUNDER: emphasizing Hopkins's acceptance of the darker as well as the more obviously beautiful side of God's presence in the world.

6–7. SINCE, THO' etc.: though God is always present in the world, that presence must be activated by man's disciplined response (*instressed*), and kept at stress and proclaimed (*stressed*). cf. 1.3 'wafting him out of it', and the end of 'Hurrahing in Harvest' (p. 68).

Stanza 6

1–8. NOT OUT OF HIS BLISS etc.: this disciplined perception of God's presence in the world does not have its source in either the beauty (*bliss*) or the disasters (*storms*) of nature. (The latter are in any case not directly caused by God.) It is, rather, something more deeply involved in history (*it rides time*).

Stanza 7

1–5. IT DATES FROM DAY etc.: it dates from Christ's actual presence in the world (*his going in Galilee*): his conception, with the *womb* forecasting the *grave*; his birth (*Manger*); and his subsequent *Passion* at Gethsemane and Calvary.

6–7. THENCE THE DISCHARGE OF IT etc.: there is its source, as though of an electrical charge, and its growth-point (*swelling*) – though these were forecast in Classical and Old Testament times (*felt before*) and are still in force (*in high flood yet*).

8 into St.8. ONLY THE HEART, BEING HARD AT BAY etc.: it is the individual in extremity who releases this recognition (*is out with it!*) of God's most essential revelation in Christ's suffering.

Stanza 8

2–3. THE BEST OR WORST/WORD LAST!: a response to the fact that it takes personal extremity to recognize Christ's suffering. This is half celebrated and half lamented by Hopkins: it is our *best word* in being a real recognition, and our *worst word* in being delayed and painful.

3–6. LUSH-KEPT PLUSH-CAPPED SLOE etc.: the sloe is the bitter plum-like fruit of the blackthorn. The image of it being bitten and burst evokes the sense of something suddenly revealing its exact nature. Here, it suggests (a) Christ's dramatic revelation of his full nature in his cruel death; (b) man's sudden realization of the significance of that death in time; and (c) man's sudden sense of the bitter-sweet fullness of his own response.

6–8. HITHER THEN, LAST OR FIRST etc.: late or soon, then, men come to recognize Christ's sacrifice – whether voluntarily and knowingly or not.

Stanza 9

3. WRING THY REBEL: continues the sense of *flush the man* from previous stanza – this time flushing out man from the kennel (*den*) of his own malice.

6–8. LIGHTNING AND LOVE etc.: the paradox is now firmly established in the poem – the co-identity of the dark and the merciful side of God's dealings with the world.

Stanza 10

1–4. WITH AN ANVIL-DING etc.: God is enjoined to *master* man either suddenly or gradually.

5–6 PAUL,/OR . . . AUSTIN: contrasting the sudden conversion of St Paul on the road to Damascus with the gentler and gradual conversion of St Augustine of Hippo (A.D. 354–430).

PART THE SECOND

Stanza 11

3. GOES DEATH ON DRUM: Death proclaims, as if beating a drum, the various forms it takes – *sword*, *flame*, *flood* etc. of the previous lines.

5. BUT WÉ DREAM etc.: man imagines that he is permanent (*rooted in earth*); but man, like that earth, is only *Dust*!

8. THE SOUR SCYTHE CRINGE: *cringe* in the archaic sense of 'cause to cringe'.

Stanza 12

3–4. TAKE SETTLER AND SEAMEN etc.: i.e. '"taking" account of the passengers and crew, and "counting" all the men and women', the number was 200.

5. NOT UNDER THY FEATHERS: not being conscious Christians (cf. *Matthew* XXIII, 37).

6. A SHOAL: on which the ship was wrecked in the Thames estuary.

6. OF A FOURTH etc.: the syntax runs 'nor guessing that it was the fate (*doom*) of a quarter of them to be drowned'.

7–8. THE BAY OF THY BLESSING etc.: the nautical meaning of *bay* leads to the later word *reeve* ('to rope together, and rope in'); but the architectural meaning of *bay* is implicit also in the word *vault*.

Stanza 13

3. SO THE SKY KEEPS: i.e. 'so the sky remains' (filled with the snow-storm) because *the infinite air is unkind*.

5–6. AND THE SEA FLINT-FLAKE etc.: 'and so also the sea remains' — sliced and raised from great depths (hence *black-backed*) by the *regular blow* of the storm'.

7. WIRY: because the snow spirals in the wind.

Stanza 14

3. COMBS: ridges.

4. KENTISH KNOCK: large sand-bank in the Thames Estuary.

7. WHORL: the screw-propeller.

8. WIND: nautical term = 'to steer'.

Stanza 15

8. SHROUDS: the rigging.

Stanza 16

6. TELL: see.

6. DANDLED: swung idly.

8. BURL: conveys the sense of full, spinning tumult.

Stanza 17

8. TOWERED: the chief sister among the five nuns drowned was reported by *The Times* as being 'a gaunt woman 6ft high'.

Stanza 18

1–2. AH, TOUCHED . . ./ARE YOU!: Hopkins addresses his own heart, moved at once to tears and joy at the nun's experience.

5. O UNTEACHABLY AFTER EVIL etc.: *after* has verbal force — though the heart seeks wilfully after evil, it is still the means for expressing truth.

6. MADRIGAL: 'sweetly lyrical'. The mystery of the tragic experience begins to centre around Hopkins's response to the reported action and words of the main nun.

7. NEVER-ELDERING REVEL etc.: the 'never-ageing joy' (as *youth* would see it) of the *river* of blood activated by the heart — an image for the unlooked-for joy (*glee*) that the tragedy contains.

Stanza 19

3. HAWLING: the form suggests both 'hauling' and 'brawling'.

4. SLOGGERING: pounding.

5. SHE THAT WEATHER: 'she in that weather . . .', by analogy with 'that day'.

6. FETCH: resource or expedient.

Stanza 20

2. COIFÈD: referring to the head-dress of the sisters' order.

3. DOUBLE A DESPERATE NAME!: the name of the country that had persecuted them, as of the ship in which they drowned.

5–8. TWO OF A TOWN etc.: Hopkins remarks on the co-existence of good and evil. St Gertrude, the thirteenth-century nun and mystic lived in a convent near Eisleben, the birthplace of Martin Luther. The latter is described as the *beast of the waste wood* because of his role as one of the main leaders of the Reformation, whose effects the Jesuits were pledged to reverse.

Stanza 21

5. ORION: the constellation named after the giant hunter.

6. UNCHANCELLING: a reference to that part of a church where the altar stands, and which is associated with sanctuary. The nuns had been in that sense 'unchancelled'. But a reference also to God 'flushing out' the individual soul (cf. stanzas 8 and 9).

8. SCROLL-LEAVED FLOWERS etc.: the *storm flakes* were, from Heaven's point of view, emblematic of the value of the suffering undergone by the nuns.

Stanza 22

1–2. FIVE! etc.: the number of nuns is emblematic of the number of wounds suffered by Christ. The word *finding* here might be rendered as 'emblem' = the device by which we 'find' the reality (hence also *cipher*). The word *sake* = the revelation of the irreducible uniqueness of Christ as a person.

3–4. MARK etc.: 'Notice that the emblem (*mark*) represents simultaneously a human nature and that nature's divine significance (*the word of it*): both *Sacrificed*.'

5–8. BUT HE SCORES IT etc.: 'But Christ marks the same wounds in blood (*in scarlet*) on those whom he has ordained before-hand as his dearest loved ones – the mark (*Stigma*), signal, and five-leaved sign (*cinquefoil token*) with which he designates the fleece of the lamb for slaughter and reddens the *rose-flake*.' (red rose = traditional Christian emblem of martyrdom).

Stanza 23

1–5. FATHER FRANCIS etc.: St Francis of Assisi, founder of the nuns' order. His body carried the stigmata, the five wounds of Christ – the symbolic pattern (*Lovescape*) of His crucifixion. The *seal of his seraph-arrival* refers to a vision St Francis had of a flaming seraph from heaven carrying in him the image of man crucified.

Stanza 24

6. THE THRONG THAT CATCHES etc.: both catching their breath and catching at something for safety.

8. THE CROSS TO HER: '(holding) the cross to her'.

8. CHRISTENS HER WILD-WORST BEST: transforms the tragedy by recognizing Christ's presence in it.

Stanza 25

2. ARCH AND ORIGINAL BREATH: Greek ἀρχή = first cause, Holy Spirit (cf. *Genesis* II, 7).

3. IS IT LOVE IN HER etc.: 'Is it that she actually wished to undergo death as Christ had done?' Hopkins begins to ask what the nun's calling on Christ actually meant.

5–6. ELSE-MINDED THEN etc.: 'in that case, Christ's disciples were very differently minded when they feared drowning' (see *Matthew*, VIII, 25).

7–8. OR IS IT THAT SHE CRIED FOR THE CROWN etc.: 'Or is it that she desired the reward (*the crown*) of martyrdom rather than the death itself, but all the more urgently because of the pain of the occasion?'

Stanza 26

1–6. FOR HOW etc.: an extended image for the contrast in the sudden access of joy after suffering. It is like a mist drifting away to reveal blue skies and the dappled freshness of spring; and later the different beauty of the sky at night.

7–8. WHAT BY YOUR MEASURE etc.: the reader is asked what his image would be for the *treasure* of Heaven — as yet unseen and unimaginable despite his *hearing* what words attempt to say.

Stanza 27

1. IT WAS NOT THESE: i.e. neither the desire for death nor the desire for Christ's crown of martyrdom as suggested in stanza 25 above.

2–5. THE JADING AND JAR etc.: 'It is the tiredness and injury suffered at the ordinary hands of life and time that makes the self-pitying heart desire release, not the more dramatic threat of danger.'

5–6. THEN FURTHER etc.: 'then again, the attraction of Christ's Passion is more comfortingly contemplated in the quietness of prayer (than in the middle of an actual emergency).'

7–8. OTHER, I GATHER etc.: 'I conclude that her motive in saying what she did was a different one.'

Stanza 28

1–5. BUT HOW SHALL I . . . etc.: the broken syntax evokes the difficulty of giving the explanation of what really did happen to the nun at that crucial point. It also parallels the panic of the actual scene.

4–5. THERE THEN! etc.: the insistence of the catalogue of names for Christ has the force almost of suggesting that He literally appeared to the nun aboard ship. The crucial word is *Ipse* – 'the very man himself'.

Stanza 29

2. SINGLE EYE!: unique and decisive in its interpretation of the event.
3. UNSHAPEABLE SHOCK NIGHT: the horror had no shape or meaning except through the nun's way of responding to it.
5–6. WORDING IT etc.: the nun's words are an 'interpretation' of the fact that all things 'express' Christ (they *are word of* Him) and are given significance only by Him (*worked by*).
7. SIMON PETER OF A SOUL: with the strength of the spiritual rock on which the church is founded (see *Matthew*, XVI, 18).
8. TARPEIAN-FAST: the Tarpeian rock was a cliff on the Capitoline hill outside Rome.

Stanza 30

3–5. WHAT WAS THE FEAST etc.: the day following the tragedy (8 December) was the Feast of the Immaculate Conception of Mary.
6. FOR SO CONCEIVĖD etc.: just as Mary herself was immaculately conceived, so also her conception of Christ was immaculate.
7–8. BIRTH OF A BRAIN etc.: the nun's experience of Christ at the point of death was itself a kind of giving birth to Christ. (The words *heard, kept,* and *uttered* suggest respectively 'conceived', 'carried', and 'gave birth to').
8. WORD: vocative addressed to Christ, in apposition to *Jesu* (ll. 1–2).

Stanza 31

2–7. BUT PITY OF THE REST etc.: Hopkins at first pities those aboard who died *comfortless*, because *unconfessed*. But he then asserts that the gentle touch of Providence in the nun made her also have the effect of 'startling' others to a realization of Christ. The *shipwrack*, then, is a *harvest* – both of the unbelieving souls aboard and of those unbelievers who hear of the nun's experience.

Stanza 32

2. YORE-FLOOD: suggesting both Noah's Deluge (*Genesis*, VII) and the waters of Creation (*Genesis*, I, 2).
5. OCEAN OF A MOTIONABLE MIND: the spiritual anarchy of man, like the waters of the world's seas, is curbed and contained by God's mastery.
6. GROUND OF BEING, AND GRANITE: continuing the image of a sea, supported from below and resisted at its margins.
8. HEEDS BUT HIDES: God's mastery is a concern that does not obviously reveal itself.
8. BODES BUT ABIDES: 'foresees but does not forestall'.

Stanza 33

3. FOR THE LINGERER etc.: '(an ark) for the lingerer with a love (that) glides . . .'.

4–5. LOWER THAN DEATH: cf. the Creed — 'He descended into Hell'.

5. A VEIN: Christ is also a 'link', through prayer, to reach those souls in Hell or Purgatory.

6–8. THE UTTERMOST MARK etc.: the syntax is 'this was the ultimate extreme (which) our giant, plunged in the suffering of death but then risen, . . . reached in the storm of his strides'.

Stanza 34

1. NEW BORN: revealed anew in the nature of the nun's death.

2. DOUBLE-NATURÈD: both human and divine.

4. MIRACLE-IN-MARY-OF-FLAME: a composite noun inscaping the paradox registered separately in the previous line — Christ, though of divine source (*heaven-flung*), was physical (*heart-fleshed*) and nurtured in Mary's womb (*maiden-furled*).

5. MID-NUMBERÈD HE: the second of the Trinity: Father, Son, and Holy Ghost.

6. NOT A DOOMS-DAY DAZZLE etc.: this revelation of Christ is not the blinding light of the Day of Judgment nor the *dark* obscurity of his original birth.

8. LET FLASH TO THE SHIRE: revealed to a particular area. Hence the emphasis in the next and final stanza on the reconversion of England.

Stanza 35

1. DAME: i.e. the nun.

1. AT OUR DOOR: the stanza makes insistent use of the words *our* and *us*, emphasizing the significance of the event for Britain.

3–4. REMEMBER US IN THE ROADS etc.: also a reference to the work of the Jesuits in England, the Reward for which would be to have 'Our King back, oh, upon English souls!'

5. EASTER: a verb — 'Let Him rise anew in us.'

'The Wreck of the Deutschland' was the first poem worked in Sprung Rhythm. Freedom in the number of syllables per line is underpinned by a regular number of stresses in each eight-lined stanza: 2-3-4-3-5-5-4-6, but with the first line changing from two to three stresses in the second part. The poem however does not make use of the extra-metrical feet which Hopkins called 'outriders' and which he used so often later (see note to 'The Wind-hover', p. 121, and other notes *passim*).

MOONRISE (June 1876) St Beuno's (*p. 61*)
A delicate evocation of a natural sight and its penetrating effect on the poet's consciousness. A MS note shows Hopkins's intention of rewriting it with one extra stress in the second half of each line.

4. MAENEFA: a darkly wooded hill rising directly behind St Beuno's College, with prehistoric burial-mounds (hence *barrow*).
5. CUSP: sharp point. One edge of the moon has not faded and appears to 'clasp' the rest of its circle.
5. FANGED: dialect verb = 'gripped'.

THE SILVER JUBILEE (1876) St Beuno's (*p. 62*)
Written as a contribution to St Beuno's celebration of Dr James Brown's twenty-fifth year as the first Roman Catholic Bishop of Shrewsbury, whose diocese included the six counties of North Wales. Hopkins also contributed Welsh and Latin poems. This English poem was set to music and sung at the celebrations.

1. NO HIGH-HUNG BELLS: because it was then forbidden to ring bells in Catholic churches.
7. THAT BUT NOW WERE SHUT: i.e. before 1850, when the Roman Catholic hierarchy was re-established for England and Wales.
14. SOME WAY SPENT: the Bishop was sixty-four, and close to retirement.

PENMAEN POOL (August 1876) Barmouth (*p. 63*)
Students from St Beuno's would spend part of the summers at Barmouth (Merionethshire), and row up the Mawddach river to visit Penmaen Pool and the George Inn, for whose Visitors' Book Hopkins wrote this poem.

7. CADAIR CLIFF: Cader Idris (2,927 ft.) to the South.
9. DYPHWYS: Diffwys (2,462 ft.) to the North.
10. GIANT'S STOOL: Cader Idris
12. TO HALVE THE BOWL: as if the personified mountains shared the *bowl* of the pool, as at a meal.
15. REPEATED TOPSYTURVY: the landscape is reflected upside-down.
17. CHARLES'S WAIN: the seven stars of the Plough, in the Great Bear constellation.
27–8. RAINDROP-ROUNDELS: interlooped circles caused by rain on the pool's surface.

GOD'S GRANDEUR (February–March 1877) St Beuno's (*p. 64*)
God's dynamic presence in and behind His created universe shames industrial man's brute materialism. Contrasted with fallen man's desolating, if superficial, effect on the natural world is the resilient freshness at the heart of nature itself.

1. CHARGED: primarily, made 'electrically' alive – hence the later images *flame, shining, lights, bright*. But also 'charged' in the sense of (a) 'rendered a debt that needs to be redeemed' (cf. the financial connotations of *spent* and *dearest* later); (b) 'challenged with' (see secondary meaning of *foil* below); and (c) 'given responsibility for'.
2. SHOOK FOIL: '*Shaken goldfoil gives off broad glares like sweet lightning and . . . owing to its zigzag dints and creasings and network of small many cornered facets, a sort of fork lightning too.*' The image also suggests a shaken rapier, consonant with meaning (b) for *charged* above.
3. THE OOZE OF OIL: *gathers, ooze* and *crushed* denote something like olive oil, with suitable 'annointing' connotations. The industrial imagery of the end of the octave, however, also makes us think of industrial oil.
4. RECK HIS ROD: 'Reck His (rod of) authority'; but also 'heed his cross' (Old English 'rood' = 'cross'). A fusion of the Old and the New Testament impressions of God.
5. GENERATIONS HAVE TROD etc.: possibly an echo of Keats's 'Ode to a Nightingale' – 'No hungry generations tread thee down'.
12. SPRINGS: the verb also suggests the noun ('springs' of water), retrospectively particularizing the claim (l. 10) that 'There lives the dearest freshness deep down things'.
13. BENT: Literally 'curved'; misshapen by human touch; financially 'crooked' (slang).
13. HOLY GHOST: see *Genesis* I, 2.

The sonnet's standard rhythm (iambic pentameter) is here counterpointed by having a freer rhythm mounted upon it.

THE STARLIGHT NIGHT (February 1877) St Beuno's (*p. 65*)
'As we drove home the stars came out thick: I leant back to look at them and my heart opening more than usual praised our Lord to and in whom all that beauty comes home' (*Journal* entry for 1874). The magical beauty of the starlit sky reminds us that the world is to be 'bought' with the coinage of the Christian faith – with prayer, patience, alms, vows – because more important than its outward splendour is the ultimate reality of Christ behind it.

Throughout the octave, and into the sestet, the images are Hopkin's terrestrial equivalents for the ways in which the starlit sky appears to him – like *fire-folk* or *bright boroughs* etc.

4. DIM WOODS: the darker background of the sky itself, against which the stars shine out. (Similarly, the *grey lawns* of the next line, with *grey* perhaps suggesting a dawning sky).

4. DIAMOND DELVES: plural of obsolete 'delf' = 'pit' or 'mine'.

5. QUICKGOLD: a coinage by analogy with 'quicksilver'.

6. WHITEBEAM . . . ABELES: respectively, the Chess Apple and White Poplar. The white undersides of their leaves are exposed when fluttered by the wind (*wind-beat*).

9. BUY THEN! BID THEN!: following on from *purchase* in the previous line, Hopkins develops the metaphor of an auctioneer highlighting the beauty of what he is selling. *What?* ('With what?') is the imagined interjection of the purchaser, who is enjoined to pay the currency of *Prayer*, *patience*, *alms*, *vows*.

10. MAY-MESS: the stars appear like clusters of blossom on the hawthorn (May) tree or on fruit trees in May. *May-mess* could also suggest 'Mary-mas', i.e. a festival for Mary. cf.'May is Mary's month' ("The May Magnificat", p. 74).

11. MEALED-WITH-YELLOW SALLOWS: *sallows* are pussy willows; the description suggests the powdery coating of their yellow flowers.

12. THESE ARE INDEED THE BARN: the sky and the stars are in fact only the outer face of reality, 'housing' the real treasures within. Apart from the thought of natural produce (*shocks* = 'sheaves' in l. 13: cf. *Matthew*, XIII, 30), the word *barn* also evokes the poor stable at Bethlehem, housing the infant Christ.

13. THIS PIECE-BRIGHT PALING: *paling* is the 'fence' of the sky, brightened piecemeal by the stars which also look like 'pieces of eight'. But *paling* also has adjectival force – growing pale as dawn comes, and in any case 'paling' in comparison with the real glories behind. These include not only Christ but Mary, physically assumed into Heaven, and the Saints (*hallows*).

Standard sonnet rhythm counterpointed; but both the octave and sestet are 'opened' with a line in sprung rhythm.

SPRING (May 1877) St Beuno's (*p.* 65)
The rich freshness of the season is seen as a reminder of an Edenic purity and as an equivalent for the same potential in a man before it is clouded and soured 'with sinning'.

2. WEEDS, IN WHEELS: denoting circular, curling growth.

3. LOOK LITTLE LOW HEAVENS: the omission of 'like' saves the phrase from being merely a precious simile.

4. RINSE AND WRING: suggest the cleansing and astringent effect of the bird's song. *Wring* also suggests 'ring'.

5. LIKE LIGHTNINGS: the switch to a visual image emphasizes the decisive suddenness of the bird's song, and the plural its repeated and echoed effects.

6. GLASSY: sharply lustrous.

6. LEAVES AND BLOOMS: either verbs, or nouns in apposition to *they*.

6. BRUSH: also as if painting or cleaning the blue of the sky.

10. STRAIN: 'the remaining essence, the surviving part of.' The word also has musical connotations. Stemming from *wring* (l. 4), there is further the sense of a 'taut' uniqueness at maximum performance.

11. HAVE, GET: Christ is urged to capture and preserve for Himself the spiritual springtime in men.

14. MOST . . . THY CHOICE etc.: *most* governs both *choice* and *worthy*: 'innocent youth is the *most choice* ('precious') and the period most worth winning'.

Standard sonnet rhythm but with 'sprung leadings' i.e. strongly stressed opening syllables to lines, challenging the iambic pattern.

IN THE VALLEY OF THE ELWY (May 1877) St Beuno's (*p.* 66) Hopkins explained the poem's essential meaning in a letter to Bridges: 'The frame of the sonnet is a rule of three sum *wrong*, thus: As the sweet smell to those kind people so the Welsh landscape is NOT to the Welsh; and then the author and principle [i.e. God] of all four terms is asked to bring the sum right.' He also noted that 'the kind of people of the sonnet were the Watsons of Shooter's Hill, nothing to do with the Elwy'.

5. CORDIAL AIR: the household's *comforting smell* (l. 3).

5. MADE THOSE KIND PEOPLE A HOOD: the object of *made* is *hood* — a covering as sheltering as a bird's *wing* over a *bevy of eggs*, or *mild nights* over the fresh growing things (*new morsels*) of spring.

8. OF COURSE: the literal, less casual meaning of the phrase — 'as a matter of course' and *of right* (l. 8).

11. ONLY. with the force of 'And yet'.

11. THE INMATE DOES NOT CORRESPOND: the native of Wales seen in terms of an 'inhabitant' (*inmate*) of the remembered house. He does not *correspond* in the sense of not *responding* to the beauty; not *corresponding* to its loveliness; and not *corresponding* ('making complete') the four terms of the pattern mentioned in Hopkins's letter, namely host-house: native-Wales. (cf. 'The Sea and the Skylark'). The poem is not an attack on the Welsh, but on the general human inability to be fit inhabitants of God's world.

14. BEING MIGHTY A MASTER etc.: Hopkins imagines a line of ordinary

syntax – 'Being a mighty master, and being a fond father' – and rearranges it to throw more separate emphases on its main parts (*mighty . . . master . . . father . . . fond*).

Standard sonnet rhythm is here both 'sprung and counterpointed': 'the most delicate and difficult business of all'. Counterpoint broadly respects the standard number of syllables, while Sprung Rhythm departs from it (cf. lines 6 and 14).

THE SEA AND THE SKYLARK (May 1877) Rhyl (*p. 66*)

The setting is Rhyl in North Wales. The theme reinforces that of 'God's Grandeur': the contrast between the prelapsarian and endless powers which nature still creates and man's unworthy betrayal of these.

2. TRENCH: 'make a penetrating, decisive noise'.

2. RAMPS: 'storms' and 'rages' against the shore.

4. MOON: under whose influence the tide works.

5. LEFT HAND, OFF LAND etc.: an example of what Hopkins called 'vowelling-off' (i.e. changing the vowels), in this case causing them to *ascend*, like the lark, up a scale. The verb *hear* has the next four finite verbs dependent on it (*ascend, whirl, pour, pelt*).

6–8. HIS RASH-FRESH RE-WINDED NEW-SKEINÈD SCORE etc.: Hopkins imagines the bird's song in visual terms. The headlong and new (*rash-fresh*) song, as having been *re-winded* on to a receptacle, is allowed to *whirl* off as from a *winch*. But also present is the idea of 'a skein of silk ribbed by having been tightly wound on a narrow card or a notched holder . . . the laps or folds are the notes or short measures and bars' of the song falling vertically to earth.

10. RING RIGHT OUT: the sounds of the sea and the skylark tell of, and expose, their sordid human opposites. The latter are also excluded, as from a 'circle' of purity.

10. TURBID: 'muddily unclear'. The word also appears in Matthew Arnold's 'Dover Beach', an interesting parallel to Hopkins's poem.

12. EARTH'S PAST PRIME: the notion of Eden, *past* because earth's freshness is now incomplete, without a corresponding freshness in man.

13–14. OUR MAKE AND MAKING BREAK etc.: industrial man, 'made' in God's image, seems bent towards not only meaningless death (*last dust*) but also his origins in primordial *slime*.

Standard sonnet rhythm, 'in parts sprung and in others counterpointed'. See note on 'In the Valley of the Elwy' above.

THE WINDHOVER (May 1877) St Beuno's (*p. 67*)
See the discussion of this sonnet in the Introduction (*p. 20*ff.) Details not included in that discussion are as follows:

1. MINION: favourite or darling
2–3. RIDING . . . STRIDING: W. H. Gardner compares the Dauphin's description of his horse in Shakespeare's *Henry V*: '*le cheval volant*, the Pegasus, *qui a les narines de feu*! When I bestride him I soar, I am a hawk: he trots the air' (III, 7).
4. RUNG UPON THE REIN: combines the sense of rising in 'rings' and the technical term ('ring on a rein') for curbing and training horses.
4. WIMPLING: 'rippling', but also curved and pleated like a nun's head-dress.
7. HEART IN HIDING: suggesting the bird's prey, but also the obscurity of religious life or a personal avoidance of exploit and danger.
11. DANGEROUS: an earlier sense of 'danger' was 'power'.
11. O MY CHEVALIER!: original sense of 'horseman', addressed both to the 'riding' bird and (through it) to the princely Christ.
13. AH MY DEAR: the phrase occurs in George Herbert's poem 'Love', addressed to the crucified Christ.
14. FALL, GALL: the two words juxtapose Adam's fall and Christ's painful redemption of it.

The first sonnet completely in Sprung Rhythm; five stresses per line, but with many 'outriding' syllables. These extra-metrical syllables find their place in a foot with a particularly strong stress, and enforce a short pause irrespective of the main caesura. Hopkins wanted this effect differentiated from that of 'falling paeonic' rhythm (a stress followed by three unstressed syllables) which also occurs here, but which he considered more easily flowing. In manuscript, he marked 'outriding' feet with loops below the line. Thus lines 2 and 3 would scan:

dŏm ŏf dáylĭght's dăuphĭn, || dăpple-dăwn-drăwn Fálcŏn, | ĭn hĭs rídĭng
ŏf tĥe róllĭng | lĕvĕl || ŭndĕrneáth hĭm | stĕady aĭr, ănd strídĭng

PIED BEAUTY (Summer 1877) St Beuno's (*p. 68*)
This central poem of praise is a call to give God glory in responding to the detailed vividness of his created things. It is based on a simple but effective paradox: the natural phenomena are chosen for their 'varying' textures or colours (see glosses on words from *dappled* onwards), but they manifest a God whose spiritual beauty is *past change*, unvarying. Compare 'As kingfishers catch fire, dragonflies draw flame' for its concentration on intense, unique detail.

1. DAPPLED: variegated.

2. BRINDED: brindled — brown streaked with other colour.

3. ROSE-MOLES: the circular, red markings on the trout's scales.

3. IN STIPPLE: '(all done) *in stipple*', marked with dots rather than lines.

5. PLOTTED AND PIECED etc.: in distinct sections, the landscape is given over to grazing (*fold* as in 'sheepfold'), or left *fallow*, or cultivated (hence *plough*).

7. COUNTER: different or varied (cf. counterpane).

7. SPARE: (like *original*) unique.

8. FICKLE: capable of change.

10. FATHERS-FORTH: this compound verb has the details of the previous three lines as its objects: 'brings them into being as contrary manifestations of Himself.'

This variation on the sonnet form is what Hopkins called a 'curtal sonnet'; that is, a reduced form of the sonnet's usual fourteen lines. It retains roughly the same proportions as the full sonnet, reducing 8 + 6 lines to 6 + 4 lines, and adding what Hopkins called a 'halfline tailpiece', whose rhyming brevity brings the sonnet to a sharp conclusion. Two other examples are 'Peace' (*p. 83*) and 'Not of all my eyes see, wandering on the world' (*p. 95*).

HURRAHING IN HARVEST (September 1877) St Beuno's (*p. 68*)
A rapturous response to the dynamic presence of God in the natural world, the sonnet 'was the outcome of half an hour of extreme enthusiasm as I walked home alone one day from fishing in the Elwy'.

1. BARBAROUS: literally (from the Latin 'barbarosus') 'bearded' or 'barbed'. The word also conveys elemental energy — 'pagan', until seen as the holy manifestation of the deeper energy of God behind.

1. STOOKS: bound sheaves of barley or wheat.

2. WIND-WALKS: the imagined tracks of winds in the sky.

3. SILK-SACK CLOUDS: Hopkins's Journal shows many examples of minutely observed and illustrated cloud effects. Here *Meal-drift* denotes the colour and texture of grain ground to powder. (The Journal describes some clouds as 'meal-white'); and as a phrase analogous with 'snow-drift', it shows the clouds being alternately shaped (*moulded*) and changed (*melted*) by the winds. The analogy with 'snow-drift' remains interestingly alive in those words *moulded* and *melted*.

5. I WALK: in such a giddily ecstatic poem, the effect is almost of treading those *wind-walks*. See the next note.

6. DOWN: verbally, 'drink'; adverbially, '*I walk . . . down*' (cf. *wind-walks* above).

6. TO GLEAN: in the sense of 'to gather', extending the harvest images.

7–8. WHAT LOOKS, WHAT LIPS etc.: a contrast with human love which returns 'less real', 'less complete and thorough' replies.

9. AZUROUS HUNG HILLS: the spaces of sky in between the curved outline of mountains are fancifully seen as, themselves, blue inverted (*hung*) hills. Pursuing the fancy, they are, as it were, God's shoulders *wielding* (i.e. 'holding' and 'carrying') the world.

10. STALLION STALWART, VERY-VIOLET-SWEET: a mixed sense of the physical strength and metaphysical sweetness of God's energy.

11–14. BUT THE BEHOLDER/WANTING etc.: it is in the event of being witnessed and responded to that these glories are activated. When that happens, it is as if the human being soars from earth.

Sonnet in Sprung Rhythm, with 'outriding' feet.

THE CAGED SKYLARK (1877) St Beuno's (*p. 69*)

A freshly dynamic treatment of the traditional concept of the soul trapped in the body's cage, the sonnet moves argumentatively towards an assertion of the ultimate freedom of the Resurrection.

1. SCANTED: deprived.

2. BONE-HOUSE: the same phrase ('ban-hus') was a typical compound in Old English verse.

3. BEYOND THE REMEMBERING etc.: have forgotten the freedom of its natural setting.

4. THIS: 'This (spirit)', a phrase parallel to 'That bird', l. 3.

5. ALOFT ON TURF: turf was sometimes placed in larks' cages.

5. OR POOR LOW STAGE: the world, the venue of man's imprisoned experience.

6. SWEETEST SPELLS: self-deluding songs.

9. THE SWEET-FOWL, SONG FOWL: the bird in its natural, free state.

12–14. MAN'S SPIRIT WILL BE FLESH-BOUND etc.: *at best* refers to man's future, resurrected condition, when the body will still be a reality, but without being an encumbrance — as light and undistressing to the spirit as the touch of a rainbow's foot on meadow-down.

Sonnet in falling paeonic rhythm (i.e. some feet being a stress followed by three unstressed syllables), but also 'sprung' and with 'outriding' feet.

THE LANTERN OUT OF DOORS (1877) St Beuno's (*p. 69*)

A meditation contrasting the limited way in which man is his brother's keeper with the endless reach of Christ's concern for each individual. The difference is pointed by the contrast between the meaning of *interest* in the second line and its repetition in the twelfth line of the sonnet. Its first use connotes something akin to idle curiosity. Its use as *Christ's interest*, however, draws on the financial sequence *rare . . . Rich . . . buys . . . interest . . . ransom.*

4. WADING LIGHT: the side-to-side motion of the carried lantern suggests resisted progress as if the darkness itself were tangible (see again *much-thick and marsh air*, l. 7).

6. MOULD: physique.

8. BUYS: 'removes them from view'.

9–10. WIND/WHAT MOST I MAY EYE AFTER: 'that which I may most carefully wind my eye after'. Hopkins admitted to Bridges the oddness of the syntactic effect. He explained, however, that the eye 'winds' in the sense of following its focus of attention – the lantern moving away and swinging from side to side.

12. CHRIST MINDS: apart from the ordinary meanings (Christ is 'concerned' and 'looks after'), there is the dialect meaning of *minds* as 'remembers'. All these meanings contrast with the cliché *out of sight is out of mind* in the previous line.

13. FOOT FÓLLOWS KÍND: His own *kind*, as a human being; but the word also has adverbial or adjectival force.

Sonnet in standard rhythm, but with a sprung effect opening line 12 and with line 9 'counterpointed'.

THE LOSS OF THE EURYDICE (April 1878) Chesterfield (*p. 70*)
The Eurydice', a training ship, was overturned by a squall from land off Ventnor, Isle of Wight, with the loss of all but two aboard. The poem can be compared with 'The Wreck of the Deutschland' in the movement from the actual tragedy to a general concern for the religious condition of England. It is, however, a slighter and less compelling poem than its more famous predecessor, and as a result its audacities of inversion and rhyme seem more vulnerable. Hopkins's confessional presence in the first part of 'The Wreck of the Deutschland', and that poem's more forthright aim of justifying the ways of God to men, are factors which make it the more complex of the two poems.

6. FURLED: buried (under sand and water).

7. FLOCKBELLS: sheepbells.

16. BOLE AND BLOOM: the ship and the men (*bole* lit. = trunk); the two words also emphasize the indiscriminate loss of men and boys, in images of achieved and potential growth.

23. BOREAS: the North Wind.

25. BEETLING BALDBRIGHT CLOUD: darkly lowering, but with tinges of light suggesting storm.

27–8. HAILROPES etc.: the image is of hail and snow swirling and winding before being released.

29. KEEP: (Carisbrook) castle, Isle of Wight.

32. BONIFACE DOWN: chalk down, behind Ventnor.

33. PRESS: technically, as much sail as a ship can carry.

34. ROYALS: the sails on the topmost royal-mast of the ship.

43. SHE WHO: i.e. the ship.

47. CHEER'S DEATH: 'the end of hope'.

50. RIGHT: a personification of Duty, which commands the captain to go down with his ship.

53–6. IT IS EVEN SEEN etc.: this stanza's meaning runs, 'Even a selfish opportunist (*time-server*), one who normally avoids responsibility, will in real extremity sacrifice everything and act correctly.'

57. SYDNEY FLETCHER: one of the two survivors.

61. AFTERDRAUGHT: the suction following the ship's sinking.

68. RIVELLING: literally 'causing to wrinkle': the man has to screw up his face in an attempt to see.

78. STRUNG BY DUTY etc.: an analogy is drawn between the parts of the dead sailor's body combining in the beauty of the whole and the trained discipline of his calling as a seaman.

87. BORN OWN: own born.

88. FAST FOUNDERING: i.e. in being lost from the Roman Catholic faith.

89–96. I MIGHT LET BYGONES BE etc.: Hopkins laments England's 'betrayals' of the Roman Catholic faith since the Reformation in the form of ruined, plundered, or unvisited shrines. He might forget these, except that he must deplore the fact that men, holy of body and quickened with life, capable of courage in death, like the members of this very crew, go themselves to ruin and damnation – because they do not die in Christ.

99. THE RIVING OFF THAT RACE: the separation of that race.

101–2. A STARLIGHT-WENDER etc.: there was a time when England was so intimate with God's truth and grace that a pilgrim on his way to the shrine of the Virgin Mary at Walsingham would call the guiding Milky Way, Walsingham Way.

103. AND ONE . . .: Hopkins explained that this curtailed reference was to Duns Scotus, the champion of the Immaculate Conception.

106. WEPT, WIFE etc.: '(O well) wept, wife; (O well) wept, sweetheart who would have liked to have been a wife'.

107. THEM: i.e. the dead sailors.

111–16. 'HOLIEST, LOVELIEST etc.': these are the supposed prayers of a bereaved mother, wife, or sweetheart.

112. SAVE MY HERO etc.: Hopkins explained that the line meant 'hero of a Saviour, be the saviour of my hero'.

114. AT THE AWFUL OVERTAKING: at the Last Judgment. The main

verbs in this stanza are past-tense imperatives (see first note to 'Henry Purcell' (*p. 128*).

117–20. NOT THAT HELL etc.: 'Not that redemption is possible for those in hell; but for souls who only *seem* to be lost, renewed prayer will bring eternal forgiveness.'

A poem in Sprung Rhythm, with three stresses in the third line of each stanza and four in the others.

THE MAY MAGNIFICAT (May 1878) Stonyhurst (*p. 74*)

'My soul magnifies the Lord': Mary's affirmation of praise on learning that the child she had conceived was Jesus lies behind this poem of praise to Mary herself. Hopkins was at the time teaching classics at Stonyhurst College, where it was a tradition to hang such verses near the statue of the Virgin. Of the feasts associated with her, the one which makes May her month seems arbitrary. Hopkins stresses the obvious suitability of May as the month of natural growth (stanzas 1–7), which reminds *us* of Mary's fruitfulness and praise (stanza 8), but also says that the month recalls the same to Mary herself.

5. CANDLEMAS: 2 February, celebrating Mary's presentation of the child Christ to the priest Simeon in the Temple (*Luke* II, 26), Jewish law indicating that this would have been at a certain period after birth.

5. LADY DAY: Feast of the Annunciation, celebrating Mary's conception of Christ by the Spirit, and fixed by the Church exactly nine months before 25 December. The dates for this and for Candlemas therefore *follow reason* (l. 3).

21. BUGLE BLUE EGGS: the colour is compared to that of the bugle (*ajuga reptans*), a woodland plant which blossoms in May.

31–2. HOW SHE DID IN HER STORED etc.: 'How she did magnify the Lord stored in her.'

39. THORP: Old English word for field or village.

41. AZURING-OVER GREYBELL: the bluebell, initially greyish, slowly turning blue (*azuring over*) as it opens.

46–7. TELLS MARY HER MIRTH etc.: 'Tells Mary to remember her mirth in the period before Christ's birth and her exultation (her Magnificat, or song of praise).'

A 'sprung' treatment of the Horatian stanza form, with four stresses in each line of the first couplet and three in each of the second.

BINSEY POPLARS (March 1879) Oxford (*p. 76*)

Binsey (Godstow) is an area of Oxford. The felling of the aspens (poplars) which lined the river there symbolized painfully for Hopkins man's destruction of the unique inscapes of nature.

1. DEAR: indicating not only delight, but also their preciousness as things which are ruined only at great cost.
1. AIRY CAGES: the outlines of the trees suggest tremulous structures within which the sunlight is *quelled* or *quenched* in the sense of being contained.
4. FOLLOWING FOLDED RANK: growing in linear sequence along the bends ('folds') of the river.
6. DANDLED: as if the aspens playfully swing their shadows.
6. SANDALLED: connoting the obvious silence of the shadows, but also possibly their interwoven visual effects.
14. SLEEK AND SEEING BALL: the *eye* of the next line.
21. ÚNSELVE: destroy the unrepeatable, *especial* identity of.

Indentation emphasizes exactly the variation from six down to two stresses per line.

DUNS SCOTUS'S OXFORD (March 1879) Oxford (*p.* 77)

This tribute to Duns Scotus's influence on Hopkins's way of looking at the world takes advantage of the fact that Scotus studied, and subsequently lectured at, Oxford. The city's suburban development is contrasted with the rural beauty, and Hopkins elegizes the time when country and town had been in a more balanced and complementary relationship. But he still breathes the same air, and can haunt the same places, as the thirteenth-century philosopher who, for Hopkins, penetrated to the essential nature of reality and the ways in which man perceives it.

2. ROOK-RACKED: Hopkins realistically includes the more raucous noise of rooks in his catalogue of the sounds of the city.
4. ENCOUNTER: semantically, the word suggests the meeting of opposites; but see next note.
4. COPED AND POISÈD POWERS: the features of town and country set each other off in a complementary balance.
5. BASE AND BRICKISH SKIRT: Hopkins lamented the fringes of red-brick suburban buildings developing in his time and which changed the direct meeting of the *grey beauty* of the city with the green country around it.
5. SOURS: (which) sours.
8. KEEPING: the sense of natural 'congruity' of the rural surroundings.
11. MOST SWAYS MY SPIRITS TO PEACE: Hopkins was grateful for Duns Scotus's example in justifying the rôle of the senses in our experience of reality.

12. REALTY: reality

12. RAREST-VEINÈD UNRAVELLER: Scotus's philosophy was renowned for its detailed and precise discriminations in desribing the nature of experience.

13. ITALY: referring to St Thomas Aquinas, the thirteenth-century philosopher, whose works are more orthodoxly central to the Catholic Church; *rival* because he devalued the knowledge that comes to man through the senses.

13. GREECE: the ultimate source of so much Western philosophy, the country of Plato and Aristotle.

14. FIRED FRANCE FOR MARY WITHOUT SPOT: Scotus lectured in Paris, and demanded the acceptance of the doctrine of the Immaculate Conception of Christ's mother. The doctrine was made central for Catholics only in 1854. This is another sense in which Scotus 'rivalled' Aquinas.

Sonnet in Sprung Rhythm, with 'outriding' feet.

HENRY PURCELL (April 1879) Oxford (*p. 78*)

Hopkins refers frequently in his correspondence to Henry Purcell (1659–95), organist at Westminster Abbey and the Chapel Royal, and Hopkins's favourite composer 'for personal preference and fellow feeling'. Generally recognized as the greatest English-born composer, Purcell was celebrated for the art of finding exact musical equivalents for the full range of human moods. Characteristically, however, Hopkins celebrates him more for the individuating than for the generalizing power of his music.

1. HAVE FAIR FALLEN: a singular imperative in the past tense, which Hopkins defended by analogy with, for example, 'Have done'. The sense is 'May good fortune have befallen you'.

2. ARCH-ESPECIAL: distinctive in the utmost sense.

3–4. WITH THE REVERSAL etc.: i.e. may the passing years have brought a reversal of the outwardly-imposed sentence under which he lay as one (en)*listed to a heresy* (Protestantism).

5–8. NOT MOOD IN HIM NOR MEANING etc.: what in the music makes the deepest impact on Hopkins is not the mood or meaning etc., which other composers might equally have fostered, but the individuating essence which proclaims the music Purcell's alone.

10. HAVE AN EYE TO THE SAKES OF HIM: 'I'll look for the distinctive qualities of his genius.'

10. QUAINT MOONMARKS: Hopkins explained, 'I mean crescent shaped markings on the quill-feathers, either in the colouring of the feather or made by the overlapping of one on another'.

11–14. SO SOME GREAT STORMFOWL: the bird is only preparing for flight, but in the act the impressiveness of his plumage is carried in upon us with a new knowledge and wonder.

12. PLUMÈD PURPLE-OF-THUNDER: this refers to the bird's colouring.

13. WUTHERING: a North country word describing the noise and movement of wind.

13. A COLOSSAL SMILE: a metaphor for the suddenly revealed impressiveness of the plumage.

14. BUT MEANING MOTION: 'only meaning to move (into flight).'

A Sprung Rhythm sonnet in Alexandrines (six stresses per line) with 'outriding' feet.

THE CANDLE INDOORS (1879) Oxford (*p.* 79)

Though not intended as such at first, this was recognized by the poet as a companion piece to 'The Lantern out of Doors' (*p.* 69). The tendency to want the work of others to be dedicated to God is checked and sobered by the realization that each person must first of all correct and dedicate himself.

2. PUTS BLISSFUL BACK: the candle's light appears to push the darkness back.

4. OR TO-FRO TENDER TRAMBEAMS TRUCKLE AT THE EYE: slender beams of light from the candle appear to advance and recede (as when one half closes and then opens the eyes). *Truckle at* means 'being subject to the influence of'. There is also an indirect comparison of the beams with tram-lines, helped by the more obvious suggestion in *truck(le)*.

6–8. A-WANTING, JUST FOR LACK/OF ANSWER etc.: 'wanting, and all the more eagerly wanting because there is no answer, that the man or woman there should be working to enlarge God's kingdom and glorify Him'.

9. COME YOU INDOORS etc.: the poet addresses himself from here on, saying that first of all there is much to improve in his own nature, where he has authority and can act on his desire to glorify God.

12. BEAM-BLIND: cf. Christ's words 'Or how wilt thou say to thy brother, let me pull the mote out of thine eye; and behold a beam is in thine own eye. Thou hypocrite, first cast out the beam out of thine own eye . . .' (*Matthew*, VII, 4).

12–13. YET TO A FAULT/IN A NEIGHBOUR DEFT-HANDED: 'yet very quick to point out a fault in someone else'.

13. THAT LIAR: that hypocrite referred to in Christ's words above.

14. SPENDSAVOUR SALT: cf. *Matthew* V, 13 – Christ calls his disciples the salt of the earth, and adds that when salt has lost its savour it is good for nothing but to be 'cast out'.

Standard sonnet rhythm counterpointed.

THE HANDSOME HEART (1879) Oxford (*p. 79*)

Written during Hopkins's year as a priest at St Aloysius's Church, in Oxford. The child's gracious answer came as a reply to Hopkins's offer to reward him and a friend for having helped Hopkins in the sacristy during Holy Week. In a letter, Hopkins explained that by the term 'handsome heart' he means beauty of character.

3. STILL PLIED AND PRESSED: i.e. for a different answer.

4. POISED: 'confident'.

5. CARRIERS: carrier pigeons.

6–8. D OFF DARKNESS etc.: pay no heed to darkness. The pigeon's homing instinct is a metaphor for the child's instinctively correct reply. In both, natural instinct is as good as long years of training.

9. MANNERLY-HEARTED!: with a heart that knows good conduct.

9. MORE THAN HANDSOME FACE: Hopkins placed beauty of character (the 'handsome heart') higher than beauty of mind, just as that was higher than beauty of body (*handsome face*).

10. OR MUSE OF MOUNTING VEIN: poetic inspiration: again a lesser thing than the 'handsome heart'.

12–13. OF HEAVEN WHAT BOON etc.: 'What favour or gift can I ask of heaven for you, that you have not already got!'

13–14. ONLY . . . O ON THAT PATH etc.: he prays only that the child should continue always in the same path.

14. BRACE STERNER THAT STRAIN: 'consolidate the firmness of that tendency and effort (*strain*)' which keeps him on the right course.

Standard sonnet rhythm counterpointed.

THE BUGLER'S FIRST COMMUNION (July 1897) Oxford (*p. 80*)

During Hopkins's period of nearly a year as a priest in Oxford, he assumed extra duties as Chaplain to the nearby Cowley Barracks. The occasion of a bugler boy from the barracks coming to his first communion at Hopkins's church enables the poet to celebrate not only the nature of the Eucharist, but the 'martial' nature of the communicant's loyalty to Christ and, indirectly, of Hopkins's own role as Jesuit priest.

5–6. AFTER A BOON etc.: 'in quest of a blessing he had asked for when I was recently there (at the barracks)'.

10. HOW FAIN I OF FEET: 'how speedily glad I was'.

11. HIS YOUNGSTER: i.e. Christ's.

12. LOW-LATCHED IN LEAF-LIGHT HOUSEL etc.: the Roman Catholic belief that Christ is actually present in the Communion wafer (for which *housel* is an archaic word).

13. THERE!: marking the actual offering of the wafer.

13–16. AND YOUR SWEETEST SENDINGS etc.: the syntax is 'may the sweetest gifts sent by you, divine heavens, befall him by this Communion'. Those gifts are then mentioned: a brave heart loving Christ; a true tongue without boast or reproach; a vital chastity with handsomeness.

17–18. ANGEL-WARDER etc.: a guardian-angel is enjoined to 'disperse (squander) the black armies from hell [that] sally to molest him'.

20. DRESS HIS DAYS etc.: an irreducible line evocative of the deft, elegant and cool discipline of a religiously committed life.

22. LIMBER: lithe, agile.

25. TREAD TUFTS OF CONSOLATION: in a precarious avoidance of depression and despair.

28. CHRIST'S ROYAL RATION: the bread and wine of the Communion.

29–30. NOT ALL SO STRAINS/US: 'not all those things which so tenses us to a heightened appreciation.'

30. FRETTED: delicately varied.

31. SWEETER ENDING: Paradise.

33. THAT SEALING SACRED OINTMENT!: the ointment which dedicated and anointed the priest's hands at his original ordination.

34. WHAT BANS OFF BAD: 'what fends off evil'.

37–40. WHOSE LEAST ME QUICKENINGS LIFT etc.: '(those sweet hopes) whose slightest stirrings raise me to joy'. Those hopes are of seeing a modern (our day) knight (Galahad) devoted to God alone. The brow and bead of being (l. 39) evokes the beads of blood-like sweat of Christ's agony in the garden of Gethsemane: the ultimate example of self-sacrifice.

40–4. THIS CHILD'S DRIFT etc.: the bugler's career, as a soldier, is already divinely determined. Hopkins therefore does not see this as a threat (disaster, l. 42) to the bugler's Christian role, yet, though bound home, might he not wander and backslide? Leaving things to God, Hopkins lays that fear by.

45–7. RECORDED ONLY etc.: 'As long as this is recorded . . .' – that Hopkins has voiced prayers which, if unheard, would shake (brandle) impenetrable (adamantine) heaven.

48. FORWARD-LIKE, BUT HOWEVER etc.: the syntax of the final line can be followed thus: 'But yet (this fear) is premature (forward-like), and it is most likely that favourable heaven heard these (pleas).'

The poem is in Sprung Rhythm, with 'overreaving' (i.e. the scansion running on from line to line). 'Outriding' (i.e. extra-metrical) syllables occur in the third foot of the last line in each stanza.

MORNING MIDDAY AND EVENING SACRIFICE (August 1879) Oxford (*p. 82*)

The freshness of youth, the strength of maturity, and the ripe wisdom of age are seen as the gifts which the three stages of man's life must give to God.

1. DIE-AWAY: denoting the gently merging colours of youth's complexion.
2. WIMPLED: curved.
6. FUMING: the *freshness* is like the smoke from incense rising to God's glory.
8. THEW: muscle.
9. TOWER: 'grow proudly' — Nature's command.
17. IN SILK-ASH KEPT FROM COOLING: the silky ash around a wood fire is a metaphor for the grey hairs underneath which the mind is still warmly active.
21. YOUR OFFERING, WITH DESPATCH, OF: 'Come, your offer of all this (the matured mind), and without delay either' (Hopkins's paraphrase).

ANDROMEDA (August 1879) Oxford (*p. 82*)

In Greek legend, Andromeda was the daughter of Cepheus, king of the Ethiopians. Her mother, Cassiopeia, had offended the Mereids (sea-maidens) with the result that Poseidon sent a sea-monster to ravage the country. The monster could be placated only by the sacrifice of Andromeda, bound to a rock. Perseus, the son of Zeus, rescued and married her. Hopkins uses Andromeda and her plight as a symbol of the Church beset by her enemies on earth, with Perseus representing Christ, the Church's spouse, rescuing His bride. This allegorical usefulness overrode Hopkins's usual objections to what he considered the triviality of classical mythology.

1. TIMES'S ANDROMEDA: the Church throughout, and in, time.
2–3. WITH NOT HER EITHER BEAUTY'S EQUAL etc.: 'unequalled in both her beauty and her injury'.
7. A WILDER BEAST FROM WEST: of the many dangers Hopkins felt in his time were threatening the true Church as he conceived it, he was probably here thinking of the new rational, liberalizing developments in theology. The extremity of his imagery can be compared to his description of Luther, the father of the Protestant Reformation, as the 'beast of the waste wood' in 'The Wreck of the Deutschland' (st. 20).
9. HER PERSEUS LINGER etc.: '(Will) her Perseus linger . . .?', a denying question.
11. FORSAKEN THAT SHE SEEMS: 'despite the fact that she seems forsaken'.

13–14. THEN TO ALIGHT DISARMING etc.: the objects of *disarming* are *thongs* and *fangs* (the thongs tying Andromeda, and the fangs of the monster).

13. NO ONE DREAMS: i.e. 'unexpectedly'.

14. WITH GORGON'S GEAR AND BAREBILL: Perseus was returning from his killing of the Gorgon Medusa, carrying her head; *barebill* = sword.

Sonnet in standard rhythm, but counterpointed by Hopkins's avowed attempt at 'a more Miltonic plainness and severity'.

PEACE (1879) Oxford (*p. 83*)

A poem which anticipates Hopkins's later contemplations on the nature of Christian patience and resilience in 'Patience, hard thing! the hard thing but to pray . . .' and 'My own heart let me more have pity on . . .', and their related companions in the form of the more extreme 'sonnets of desolation' of the Irish period.

2. UNDER BE: the inversion makes *under* more a part of the verb than an adverb. *cf.* 'understand'.

4. TO OWN MY HEART: inversion of 'To my own heart': he will not lie to his own heart. But the inversion creates another meaning: he will not lie in order to appear to be in independent control of (*to own*) his emotions.

5. PIECEMEAL PEACE: intermittent peace.

5. PURE PEACE: *pure* not only in the sense of 'unadulterated', but also 'total', 'nothing but' peace.

6. WARS: inner, spiritual conflicts.

6. THE DEATH OF IT: i.e. 'of peace itself'.

7. REAVING PEACE: not a vocative addressed to Peace, but a present-participial phrase: 'since my Lord "plunders" or "carries off" Peace, He should leave at least some good to take its place'.

8. PATIENCE: not Peace itself, but an intermediary condition necessary for Peace; the basic meaning of 'the acceptance of suffering' is relevant – hence the adjective *exquisite*, 'acute', 'keen'.

9. PLUMES TO PEACE: the notion of 'gaining a covering' and 'growing naturally'. By comparison, Patience is something barer and more unaccommodated.

11. BROOD AND SIT: a Biblical reference to the Spirit (*Genesis* I, 2) brooding on the surface of the waters, hatching the Creation itself. This is the sense in which it is a condition that *comes with work to do* (1. 10).

This is a 'curtal sonnet': see notes on 'Pied Beauty' (*p. 122*). The metre is 'standard Alexandrines' (six iambic feet per line).

AT THE WEDDING MARCH (October 1879) Bedford Leigh, Lancashire (p. 83)
The priest prays inwardly for the future of a pair he has just joined in marriage.

1. HANG YOUR HEAD: 'decorate (with *honour*), as with a garland'.
3. LISSOME: gracefully lithe.
3. SCIONS: literally, young shoots from parent plant: offspring.
6. DÉEPER THAN DIVINED: deeper than you could have imagined.
8. DEAR CHARITY, / . . . FAST BIND: cf. *Colossians* III.
10. I TO HIM TURN: to God or Christ, who makes the bond of marriage extend beyond time; hence *immortal years*.

The poem is in Sprung Rhythm, with four stresses to a line.

FELIX RANDAL (April 1880) Liverpool (*p. 84*)
The subject was a blacksmith (*farrier*), probably one of Hopkins's parishioners at Leigh in Lancashire, where the poet was priest for three months at the end of 1879. The poem was, however, written at Liverpool where Hopkins found his priestly duties less rewarding. He measures God's gift of grace in the Eucharist (in which each man is as a receptive child) against the tribute also due to the blacksmith's former physical strength, before 'sickness broke him'.

3. TILL TIME WHEN: 'till the time came when . . .'
5. SICKNESS BROKE HIM: with the slight suggestion of animal power being curbed. cf. note on *powerful amidst peers* below.
6. A HEAVENLIER HEART: a heart directed more towards heavenly things.
7. OUR SWEET REPRIEVE AND RANSOM: the salvation offered through the Holy Communion.
8. ALL ROAD EVER: colloquial Lancashire expression meaning 'in whatever way'.
9. US TOO IT ENDEARS: this is essentially a priest's poem: illness not only 'draws affection' from the priest, but makes his rôle as priest 'precious'.
11. CHILD: the parishioner's spiritual relationship to the priest.
12. HOW FAR FROM THEN FORETHOUGHT OF etc.: 'How far were your years of active life from any forethought of their cessation in sickness and death.'
13. RANDOM: suggests both the cluttered untidiness of the forge and possibly the random sparks from the fire. Architecturally, the term denotes rough stone-work.
13. POWERFUL AMIDST PEERS: his *peers* could be either other blacksmiths or the horses themselves, matching his *big-boned* stature.
14. FETTLE: as a verb, dialect: 'to condition and trim'.

14. SANDAL: i.e. horseshoe.

A poem in Sprung Rhythm, with six stresses to a line and many 'outriding' feet.

BROTHERS (August 1880) Hampstead (*p. 85*)

Hopkins had had the example of Wordsworth's simpler poems in mind here, though recognizing Wordsworth's radically different approach to language. Nonetheless, the poem's delight in a simple anecdote for the way it reveals primary human emotions of moral value, makes Wordsworth an interesting comparison. The incident occurred during Hopkins's period as sub-minister at Mount St Mary's College, Chesterfield.

5. SHROVETIDE: the period when penitents were 'shriven' (cleansed) of sin, in readiness for the Lenten fast which directly followed.
15. BY MEANWHILES: 'in short, unnoticed periods'.
18. LOST IN JACK: unselfconsciously possessed by the expectation of his brother's entry on stage.
22. TRUTH'S TOKENS TRICKS LIKE THESE: gestures like these are signs of unfeigned feelings.
38. FRAMED IN FAULT: given a distorted shape by man's Original Sin.
39. THERE'S SALT: i.e. to heal Nature's wounds.

The poem is in Sprung Rhythm, with three stresses to a line, and with no 'overreaving' (i.e. no metrical continuation from line to line).

SPRING AND FALL (September 1880) Lydiate, Lancashire (*p. 86*)

Not founded on any real incident, nor concerning any real child or place, the poem articulates the perennial theme of transience, linked to the theme of human growth from innocence to experience. Hopkins's period at Liverpool, where this poem was written, was one marked often by depression and despair. Human failings, and desolating work in sordid industrial conditions, perhaps gain an indirect and impersonal expression in this address 'to a young child'.

1. GOLDENGROVE: a fairly common place-name throughout Britain.
2. UNLEAVING: i.e. losing its leaves in autumn.
6. IT WILL COME TO SUCH SIGHTS COLDER: 'it will come colder (less emotionally) to such sights', but also 'it will come to such colder sights than this'. Both meanings emphasize the poem's assertion that it is not nature's death that we really mourn.
8. WANWOOD: the coinage suggests forests dead and colourless.
8. LEAFMEAL: *meal* evokes the brown-golden colour of the fallen leaves,

while the whole coinage is by analogy with 'piecemeal' i.e. 'fallen leaf-by-leaf'.

9. AND YET YOU WÍLL WEEP AND KNOW WHY: the *yet* is in contradiction of *nor spare a sigh* (1.7). The child will in future years know that what she mourns is human mortality.

9–12. NOW NO MATTER, CHILD, THE NAME etc.: to *name* the real sources of grief would be of no significance to the child at present because, though they are the sources (*springs*) of all grief, these intimations of human mortality come at present from sub-verbal and sub-mental levels of understanding – those of the *heart* and spirit (*ghost*).

14. BLIGHT: suitably, in the context, suggestive of organic disease, the word also refers to the fact that death is the inevitable legacy of man's Fallen condition.

A poem in Sprung Rhythm, with four stresses to a line. In this shorter measure, Hopkins thought it important that a falling rhythm at the end of one line should be followed by a 'sprung head' (i.e. a stressed first syllable) in the next.

INVERSNAID (September 1881) (*p. 87*)
Hopkins had briefly visited Inversnaid, near Loch Lomond in Scotland, and the present poem is, in the linguistic as well as the visual sense, poetry of place. It also drew, however, on stored images from much earlier notebooks, and expressed the general, deep-seated respect for natural wildness out of the reach of man and society's influence, which alone is really desolating. In a letter to Bridges he expressed fears of 'the decline of wild nature'.

1, 2. BURN: (Scots) stream.

3. IN COOP AND IN COMB: respectively, the convex and concave 'rib' effects of water running over stones.

4. FLUTES: 'makes grooves in': its subject is *burn*, its object *the fleece of his foam*.

5. WINDPUFF-BONNET OF FÁWN-FRÓTH: the light vapour caused by the descent of a waterfall into a pool.

6. TWINDLES: combining the sense of 'twists' and 'dwindles'.

9. DEGGED: (Lancashire dialect) 'sprinkled'.

10. GROINS OF THE BRAES: the depressions between hillsides, carved or followed by the stream.

11. HEATHPACKS: heather clumps.

11. FLITCHES: tufts.

12. BEADBONNY ASH: the adjective might refer to the purplish, almost knobbly clusters of the ordinary ash tree's flowers, or the bright scarlet berries of the Mountain Ash.

'AS KINGFISHERS CATCH FIRE, DRAGONFLIES DRAW FLAME' (1881) (*p. 87*)

This sonnet is one of the most forthright expressions of Hopkins's belief in what Duns Scotus called 'haecceitas' – the individual and unique 'thisness' of every item in the created world. Every action or effect is the manifestation of unique inner selfhood. Christian man finds his context in such a world, but the poem implies an even greater value ('I say more . . .', l. 9) in man's self-revelation because that is a conscious act, and Hopkins keeps the diction of real value – *more*, *just*, *grace*, *Christ*, *lovely* – for the description of man in the sestet.

1. CATCH FIRE . . . DRAW FLAME: by reflecting the sunlight.
2. TUMBLED OVER RIM IN ROUNDY WELLS: the absence of commas gives these words the force of a single compound adjective describing *stones*.
3. TUCKED: 'plucked'.
4. BOW: denoting both the bell's shape and its clapper.
6. THAT BEING INDOORS EACH ONE DWELLS: 'that "being" which dwells indoors in each one thing'.
7. SELVES – GOES ITSELF: 'registers its individual identity'; *goes* also has the force of 'speaks' or 'utters' (cf. *goes Death on drum*, 'The Wreck of the Deutschland' st. 11).
8. FOR THAT I CAME: subtly reminiscent of Christ's words 'I came that you might have life . . .' (*John* X, 10).
9. JUSTICES: 'manifests the inner justness of his nature'.
10. KÉEPS GRÁCE: etc.: 'pays due regard to grace' – which in turn *keeps all his goings graces*.
11. ACTS: like *plays* in the next line, not in the sense of 'acting out' a part, but 'expressing the reality of'. Elsewhere Hopkins wrote, 'It is as if a man said: That is Christ playing at me and me playing at Christ, only that it is no play but truth; that is Christ *being me* and me being Christ.'
13–14. LOVELY IN LIMBS etc.: Christ's beauty is made attractive to God by its manifestation through the limbs, the eyes and features of other men.

A sonnet in Sprung Rhythm, with five stresses to a line.

RIBBLESDALE (1882) Stonyhurst (*p. 88*)

In September 1882 Hopkins began a spell of teaching at Stonyhurst College, near Blackburn in Lancashire, a public school staffed almost entirely by Jesuits. He had previously spent three years there studying Philosophy (1869–72) and it was a place which much impressed him with its beautiful moorland scenery. But the later period at Stonyhurst was marked by ailments and depression – a background, to some degree, to this poem's contrast between God's created beauties and man's grudging and ruinous response. A Latin epigraph from Paul's Epistle to the Romans (VIII, 19–20), in the MSS. of the poem speaks of future freedom from man-and-nature's fallen bondage; but Hopkins's sonnet still ends darkly.

1. WITH LEAVÈS THRONG: a Lancashire use of *throng* as adjective ('crowded with').
2. LOUCHÈD: Hopkins explained that he meant 'slouched' or 'slouching'.
4. THAT CANST BUT ONLY BE etc.: nature praises God by 'being' rather than consciously 'doing' — but it is as least an eternal praise.
5–6. STRONG/THY PLEA: i.e. nature's deserved right to God's attention.
6–7. WHO DEALT . . . DOWN: who created; and sustains (*nay does now deal*).
7. REEL: meander.
8. AND O'ER GIVES ALL: 'and gives everything over (*to rack or wrong*)'.
9–10. AND WHAT IS EARTH'S EYE etc.: earth's unconscious praise can be made sensitive, articulate, and felt only in man.
10. DOGGED: grimly persistent.
12. TO THRIFTLESS REAVE: 'to plunder wastefully'.
13–14. THIS BIDS WEAR/EARTH etc.: this blind selfishness in man bids earth wear an expression of care etc.

The standard sonnet rhythm is very markedly counterpointed.

THE LEADEN ECHO AND THE GOLDEN ECHO (finished October 1882) Stonyhurst (*p. 89*)

The poem was planned as a chorus in Hopkins's unfinished drama, 'St Winefred's Well', started in October 1879. According to the later middle-ages legend, St Winefred was a niece of St Beuno. Her head was cut off by a chieftain's son, Caradoc, whose sexual advances she had resisted. Beuno restored the head to her body, and where the head had fallen (at Holywell, near St Beuno's) a spring of healing water appeared. King Henry VII's mother, Lady Margaret Beaufort, had the well enclosed by a stone building, and it remains a place of pilgrimage. Here, a despairing meditation on the transience of beauty is countered by the notion that beauty, to be preserved, must be selflessly sacrificed to 'God, beauty's self and beauty's giver'.

THE LEADEN ECHO

1. BOW OR BROOCH etc.: the catalogue stresses beauty as something that can be physically preserved or lost, and also emphasizes a feminine context (*bow, braid, lace* etc.).

3–4. Ó IS THERE NO FROWNING . . . DOWN?: the last two words go together, i.e. *frowning down* the wrinkles, smoothing them out.

4. MESSENGERS: i.e. the advance signs of age. cf. George Herbert's poem 'The Forerunners'.

8. WISDOM IS EARLY TO DESPAIR: wisdom is the early acceptance of the fact that beauty vanishes.

THE GOLDEN ECHO

17. SPARE!: i.e. 'leave off!, listen!'

26. WIMPLED-WATER-DIMPLED: 'dimpled like wimpled water'. The phrase describes *face*.

27. FLEECE OF BEAUTY: Hopkins explained that *fleece* should convey the sense of velvet texture.

28. NEVER FLEETS MÓRE: this verb has, as its composite subject, the catalogue which begins with *whatever's prized* in line 26.

34. BEAUTY-IN-THE-GHOST: 'beauty of the spirit'.

35. BEAUTY'S SELF AND BEAUTY'S GIVER: physical beauty has its identity and reality, and its source, in the fuller beauty of God.

37. HAIR OF THE HEAD, NUMBERED: an allusion to *Matthew* X, 30 and *Luke* XII, 7.

38–41. WHAT HE HAD LIGHTHANDED LEFT etc.: the image informing these lines is that of a seed carelessly thrown into dull earth (*surly . . . mould*): it will have germinated and grown, unbeknown to us on *this side* of the grave, and producing a copious harvest on that other side, in heaven. There is a reference in the word *hundredfold* to Christ's words in *Matthew* XIX, 29.

42. CARE-COILED: 'disturbed by care'.

42. SO FAGGED, SO FASHED, SO COGGED: 'so exhausted, so care-worn, so deluded'. *fashed* is a Scots dialect word and *cogged* an archaic word, with implications of the fraudulent manipulation of dice in gambling.

45. FAR WITH FONDER A CARE: 'with a far fonder care'.

Hopkins's delight in 'sprung' movement is in one sense given freer rein here, without keeping to a patterned number of stresses per line; but the long lines put even more to the test his claim that 'everything is weighed and timed in them'.

THE BLESSED VIRGIN COMPARED TO THE AIR WE BREATHE (May 1883) Stonyhurst (*p. 91*)

Written as a 'Maypiece' in honour of the Virgin Mary, according to the custom at Stonyhurst (cf. 'The May Magnificat'), this poem's extended comparison is reminiscent of the imaginative, intellectually sustained, conceits of seventeenth-century 'Metaphysical' verse. Just as the air sustains life and moderates the heat of the sun, so the Virgin is a medium for man's spiritual life and a mediator of God's glory and power.

4. GIRDLES: 'encircles'.

5. FRAILEST-FLIXED: 'delicately fleeced'.

7. RIDDLES: 'inter-penetrates'.

16. MINDS ME: 'reminds me'.

22. BUT MOTHERS EACH NEW GRACE: grace, the source of holiness, is God's gift, but mediated through Mary.

24. MARY IMMACULATE: Hopkins believed Mary herself to have been born by Immaculate Conception: a dogma made central for Roman Catholics by papal proclamation in 1854.

25. MERELY A WOMAN: 'only' but also 'completely' a woman.

36–7. THE SAME/IS MARY: i.e. mercy *is* Mary.

40–1. LET DISPENSE/HER PRAYERS: i.e. 'let her prayers dispense . . .'.

43. THE SWEET ALMS' SELF IS HER: Mary is not only the giver, but the gift itself (of mercy).

48. GHOSTLY GOOD: 'spiritual benefit'.

51–2. LAYING . . . /THE DEATHDANCE: terminating or mitigating the physical tendency towards death.

53–4. YET NO PART BUT . . .: Mary plays her *part* (l. 49), but in reality this is Christ's saving role that is enacted.

56–72. HE DOES TAKE FRESH AND FRESH etc.: Christ's physical birth is in the past, but he is spiritually and endlessly reborn now in each man. *Nazareth* and *Bethlem* denote (the places of) Christ's conception and birth. Meditation upon Biblical scenes, for their renewing spiritual energies, was central to Jesuits as part of the Ignatian spiritual exercises.

79–80. SAPPHIRE-SHOT,/CHARGED, STEEPED: *sapphire* qualifies all these three adjectives for *sky*.

80–1. WILL NOT/STAIN LIGHT: from here to the end of the verse-paragraph is developed the analogous fact that the blueness of the air enhances rather than obscures the colours and definition of other things, and of sunlight itself. It similarly mitigates the glare of the sun. Without it, the sun would blind and create a surrounding blackness against which other stars would also be harshly visible.

103. SO GOD WAS GOD OF OLD: the harsh sun has been an analogy for the Old Testament conception of God, now contrasted with the tenderer New Testament Nativity.

106. DAYSTAR: the sun, used thus as image for Christ in 2 *Peter* I, 19.

119. FROWARD: perverse.

The poem is in Sprung Rhythm, with three stresses to a line.

'NOT OF ALL MY EYES SEE, WANDERING ON THE WORLD' (1885) (*p. 95*)

In this form, the earlier of two versions, the poem is another curtal sonnet. (See notes on 'Pied Beauty', *p. 122*.)

7. TABOUR: 'tap lightly', as on a drum.
9. MELLS: 'mixes'.

SPELT FROM SIBYL'S LEAVES (1884–85) (*p. 95*)

Just as the Sibyl deciphered the judgment of the gods from natural signs, Hopkins here prefigures God's judgment in a description of evening first obliterating and then transforming the world usually seen by day. It brings in a new order which emphasizes, in its 'black' and 'white', the clear understanding of 'wrong' and 'right' by which man is urged to live.

1. EARTHLESS: because as if dissolving the material world, and being of a different order of reality from it.
1. EQUAL: in one sense, *equal* to the task of transformation.
1. ATTUNEABLE: capable of 'harmonizing' two different dimensions.
3–4. HER FOND YELLOW HORNLIGHT etc.: the rays of the sun, *wound to the west* at sunset, give way to the *hoarlight* of the period before the stars appear (hence *hollow*); but both *waste* in the sense of fading and giving way to the different light when the stars do appear.
4–5. EARLIEST STARS, EARL-STARS etc.: the earliest stars then give way to the appearance of the full constellations (*stars principal*) which *overbend* or dominate, revealing the face of heaven – *fire-featuring* it.
5–7. HER BEING HAS UNBOUND etc.: the *being* of earth is its unique 'dappled' variety: this is now dissolving, merging and losing separate identity. The dialect word *throughther* (l. 6) = 'through each other'.
7. HEART, YOU ROUND ME RIGHT: the obsolete verb *round* = 'warn' or 'whisper'.
9. BEAK-LEAVED BOUGHS: because the leaves are silhouetted like beaks against the sky.
9. DAMASK: 'mark with patterns'.
10–14. ÓUR TALE, O ÓUR ORACLE! etc.: Hopkins remarks the lesson implicit in a scene which has changed the world to black and white. The final lines of the poem can be loosely paraphrased: 'Let life, once passed, wind off all her once varied patterns on to two spools; let her divide and pen that variety in two flocks representing in the end only two things – right and wrong; let her pay attention only to these two divisions; let her be aware of a world to come where these are the only two divisions which count; let her be aware of a punishment that will take the form of an eternal living with only the tormented self, divorced from God.'

Hopkins called this 'the longest sonnet ever made'. It is in Sprung Rhythm, with eight stresses to a line.

TO WHAT SERVES MORTAL BEAUTY? (August 1885) (*p. 96*)

The poem places human physical beauty in relation, on the one hand, to the dangers that can vulgarize it (its temptations to lustful feelings and to vain self-regard), and on the other to its nature as God's gift and the medium of a more important spiritual and inner beauty. These can be compared to similar discriminations in the poem 'The Handsome Heart' (*p. 79*).

1. DANGEROUS: in the sense of exciting only physical passion.
2. THE O-SEAL-THAT-SO FEATURE: the beauty that would make one want to capture and preserve (*seal*) it for all time, as in art.
2–3. FLUNG PROUDER FORM/THAN PURCELL TUNE etc.: the difference between the self-regarding display of beauty and the unselfconscious (but unique) identity expressed in Purcell's music. For the latter, see the sonnet 'Henry Purcell' (*p. 78*).
3. SEE: IT DOES THIS: the poem begins to answer its opening question.
3–4. KEEPS WARM/MEN'S WITS TO THE THINGS THAT ARE: keeps men's understanding alive to the most important realities, to genuine spiritual 'being'.
4–5. A GLANCE/MASTER MORE MAY: 'may bring about more (than a *gaze*)'. Inner identity 'glances' or *flashes* (1. 11). Similarly, it calls for deft alertness rather than the fuller *gaze* demanded by physical beauty alone.
6–8. THOSE LOVELY LADS etc.: the reference is to some British boys seen at a Roman slave-market by Pope Gregory I (*c.* 590–604 A.D.). Their beauty prompted him to send Augustine (later St Augustine of Canterbury) to win England to Christianity.
10. LOVE'S WORTHIEST, WERE ALL KNOWN: 'the things that are worthiest of love, taking into account inner as well as outer realities'.
11. SELVES: 'inner identities'.
12–13. OWN/HOME AT HEART, etc.: 'recognize, in your own heart, that (physical beauty) is the sweet gift of heaven'.
14. WISH THAT THOUGH, WISH ALL, etc.: 'wish for that beautiful person, and for all humans, the better beauty of God's grace'.

A sonnet in alexandrines (six stresses per line) but with its standard rhythm very heavily stressed: Hopkins placed markings over juxtaposed syllables, indicating that they had equal stress in recitation although only one carried the 'metrical' stress.

'YES. WHY DO WE ALL, SEEING OF A SOLDIER, BLESS HIM?' (August 1885) Clongowes (*p. 97*)

Our respect for soldiers and sailors springs from our hope that the disciplined valour of their calling is also true of their character. As usual, the subject appeals to the spiritually militant nature of Hopkins's Jesuit training, and leads to a picture of Christ also as the King of manly struggle.

2. REDCOATS: British soldier uniforms were red.
2. TARS: obsolete colloquial term for 'sailors'.
3. HERE IT IS: 'this is the answer'.
4. PROUD: refers to the heart which *calls the calling manly*.
6. AND SCARLET WEAR etc.: '(And fain will find) scarlet wear (to) express the spirit of war there'.
10. REEVE: 'to pass through and secure'.
10. THERE HE BIDES: i.e. in Heaven.
13. SO GOD-MADE-FLESH DOES TOO: just as man's best actions emulate Christ, so Incarnate God-in-Christ acted, and would act, fully as a man.
14. WERE I COME O'ER AGAIN: i.e. were He to become man on earth again: *it should be this* same pattern he would follow.

A sonnet in alexandrines (six stresses per line), heavily stressed — with additional strong stresses not counting metrically.

THE IRISH 'SONNETS OF DESOLATION'

The term 'Sonnets of Desolation' or 'Terrible Sonnets' can conveniently refer to the six sonnets which now follow, despite the fact that the poems themselves represent varying degrees of the feeling of hopelessness, and that 'Patience, hard thing!' and 'My own heart let me more have pity on' represent a calm corrective to the predicament described. Moreover, the traumas of faith on which they draw gained equally memorable expression as early as the first part of 'The Wreck of the Deutschland'. Nevertheless, these shorter expressions of a mood Hopkins was particularly prone to during the period in Ireland do come together in the reader's mind — and in ways that could also include 'Spelt from Sibyl's Leaves' (p. 95) and 'Thou art indeed just, Lord, if I contend' (p. 104).

'NOT, I'LL NOT, CARRION COMFORT, DESPAIR, NOT FEAST ON THEE' (1885) (*p. 97*)

1. CARRION COMFORT: Despair seen as dead emotion, off which the poet would dangerously feed.
5. O THOU TERRIBLE: spoken to Christ.

5. RUDE ON ME: adverbial phrase (*rudely on me*) governing the verb *rock* in next line.
6. LIONLIMB: cf. *Job* X, 16.
7. DARKSOME: 'gloomy'.
7. FAN: the image is of winnowing, with a scoop used to throw the grain against the wind, thus separating it from the chaff.
10. COIL: 'bustle', 'confusion'.
10. I KISSED THE ROD: the rod of God's authority, but also the 'rood' (cross) of Christ's sacrifice.
12. THE HERO: Christ.
13. THAT NIGHT, THAT YEAR: cf. *'But where I say/Hours I mean years, mean life'* ('I wake and feel the fell of dark, not day', *p.* 99).

A Sprung Rhythm sonnet, with six stresses to a line and several 'outriding' feet.

'NO WORST, THERE IS NONE. PITCHED PAST PITCH OF GRIEF' (1885) (*p. 98*)
1. NO WORST: one cannot call an experience the *worst* when, always, worse experiences succeed.
1. PITCHED PAST PITCH OF GRIEF: *pitch* combines 'being thrown', blackness, and the experience of a highly-strung consciousness.
2. SCHOOLED AT FOREPANGS: the *pangs* (pains) learn their power from previous ones (*forepangs*).
3. COMFORTER: addressed to the Holy Ghost.
5. HERDS-LONG: driven and crowded endlessly together.
8. FELL: Fury shouts its aim of being both 'swift' and 'terrible'.
8. FORCE: perforce.
9–10. CLIFFS OF FALL/FRIGHTFUL: an image which – with the later ones of storm, poor shelter and sleep – seems to distil the experience of Shakespeare's *King Lear*. cf. Gloucester thinking himself at Dover cliffs in that play (IV, vi).
13–14. A COMFORT etc.: the vulnerable comfort of painful life not being endless, of sleep closing each cruel day.

Standard sonnet rhythm (i.e. iambic pentameter), but with strong Sprung Rhythm effects.

'TO SEEM THE STRANGER LIES MY LOT, MY LIFE' (1885) (*p. 98*)
Hopkins's conversion had meant alienation from family and from Anglican England. His move to Ireland now brought literal separation. He recognized

that his mood reflected a physical as well as spiritual tiredness, which might have remained unchanged even outside Ireland, but the patriotic note struck in this sonnet reflects his complex experience of the Irish political situation at that time. The Irish Jesuits supported Irish home rule, a thing which Hopkins could only with difficulty do because of his deep love for England, his hopes in any case for England's reconversion to Roman Catholicism, and his natural respect for authority.

3. ARE IN CHRIST NOT NEAR: his family was staunchly Anglican, and had resisted and lamented his conversion.

7. WERE I PLEADING: i.e. about the tragedy of the Irish situation. Hopkins's English patriotism did not exclude real sorrow at England's neglect and mismanagement of Ireland.

8 BUT BY WHERE WARS ARE RIFE: 'where only conflicts multiply'.

9–10. A THIRD/REMOVE: already removed from his family and from England, he feels alienated also from the Catholic Church in Ireland over the Home Rule question.

11–13. ONLY WHAT WORD/WISEST etc.: the force of *only* is 'except that . . .'.

14. LEAVES ME A LONELY BEGAN: *began* as a noun ('one who only began, and did not finish') is possibly by analogy with 'an also-ran'.

Standard sonnet rhythm (i.e. iambic pentameter), but very heavily counterpointed in the second half of the octave.

'I WAKE AND FEEL THE FELL OF DARK, NOT DAY' (1885)
(*p.* 99)

1. THE FELL OF DARK: as a noun, *fell* = the hairy skin of an animal. But the word also has the adjectival force of 'fierce, terrible' and the verbal force of 'fall' ('the fall of dark', 'the dark which fell').

4. AND MORE MUST: he must experience more horror until literal or spiritual daylight come.

7–8. CRIES LIKE DEAD LETTERS etc.: the spiritual state of feeling totally separated from God.

10. MY TASTE WAS ME: the language of the sestet registers the spiritual desolation as an unrelieved neurotic awareness of the egotistic, physical self.

11. BONES BUILT IN ME etc.: '*Bones built* (the curse) *in me, flesh filled* (the curse), *blood brimmed the curse*'.

12. SELFYEAST OF SPIRIT etc.: the notion that the spirit should leaven or transform the *dull dough* of physical existence; but, being embroiled in a total selfness, it only *sours*.

14. BUT WORSE: the predicament of those who, without belief, are really damned or *lost*.

Standard sonnet rhythm (i.e. iambic pentameter), but with freely dramatic concentration of stresses at times.

'PATIENCE, HARD THING! THE HARD THING BUT TO PRAY' (1885) (*p. 99*)

1–4. BUT TO PRAY etc.: it is hard 'even to pray for' Patience, as the next three lines explain: because the prayer should really involve an acceptance of the things which give Patience its real meaning (*war*, *wounds*, *weary times* and *tasks* etc.).

10. TO BRUISE THEM DEARER: *dearer* (archaic) = 'more grievously'.

14. COMBS: honeycombs.

Standard sonnet rhythm, but with marked counterpointing at times.

'MY OWN HEART LET ME MORE HAVE PITY ON' (1885) (*p. 100*)

5–8. I CAST FOR COMFORT etc.: '*I cast for comfort I can no more get /By groping round my comfortless* (world), *than blind/Eyes in their dark* (world) *can* (find) *day or thirst can find* etc.' the last reference seems an echo of Coleridge's Ancient Mariner: 'water, water everywhere, but not a drop to drink'.

9. POOR JACKSELF: his own common self.

11–12. LET JOY SIZE etc.: 'let joy grow and strengthen at a time and occasion to be determined by God'.

12–13. WHOSE SMILE/'S NOT WRUNG: 'whose favour is not to be forced'.

13–14. AS SKIES/BETWEENPIE MOUNTAINS: *Betweenpie* is a verb – 'as skies dapple the space between two mountains'.

14. LIGHTS: its subject is God's *smile* (l. 12).

The standard sonnet rhythm of the octave is much less discernible in the sestet.

TOM'S GARLAND (September 1887) Dromore (*p. 101*)

A companion piece to 'Harry Ploughman' (*p. 101*). Its theme is the view of the commonwealth or well-ordered society as being like the body of one man, with a proper station and function to each part, the lowliest taking its pride from 'the honour that belongs to the whole'. Hopkins's explanation to Bridges refers to St Paul, Plato, and Hobbes as authority for such a view. One also remembers Menenius's speech to the plebeians in Shakespeare's *Coriolanus*

(I, i), and many other individual images are also borrowed from that play. For Hopkins, social anarchy is not the result of low status but of people finding no place at all in the body-politic.

The following is a close paraphrase of the poem's development:

Tom – his boots garlanded with squat and surly steel (nails); then sturdy Dick, Tom's fellow-labourer, fallow or idle now after work, sets aside his pick and strides homewards, striking sparks from the ground with his boots. Tom, a navvy at ease with the world, thinks now only of supper and bed. His is a low lot but (being one who need never feel hunger, who is seldom sick, seldomer heartsore, who treads invulnerably through the thousands of thorns that thoughts can be) he swings or dismisses it as a light matter. 'I waste no time thinking of the Commonweal! I would lack high status even in a state where all had bread: What! belonging to a well-ordered country is itself honour enough in all of us – whether one is the lordly head, encircled by the stars, or the mighty foot that disfigures the mother-earth'. But there are those who are given no satisfaction in either mind or bodily strength; who neither carry the dangerous adornment of wealth nor labour safely at the lower levels; cast out from the glory of life, and its comfort, from everything; with no individuality nor place in the world's general good; devoid of both wealth and honest labour; anxiety, however, they do have a share in – and this, when it becomes Despair, makes them lazy curs; when it becomes Rage, it makes them something worse, human wolves; and their packs infest the age.

This 'caudal' or 'caudated' sonnet has two 'codas' or additions to the usual fourteen lines: the three lines beginning 'Undenizened . . .' and those beginning 'In both . . .' See also That Nature is a Heraclitean Fire' (p. 102).

Standard sonnet rhythm (iambic pentameter), but with 'hurried' feet crowding up to four syllables into the time of one.

HARRY PLOUGHMAN (September 1887) Dromore (p. 101)
Conceived at the same time, this poem and the more overtly political 'Tom's Garland' (p. 101) were regarded by Hopkins as companion pieces. They celebrate respectively a rural and an urban labourer. Hopkins on reflection considered both poems technically over-wrought, but emphasized the importance of reading-aloud for an understanding of them. Harry Ploughman is realized purely in terms of physique and the physical effort that his work entails – though not reductively, and not without a firm enobling power in the imagery.

1–2. WITH A BROTH OF GOLDFISH FLUE etc.: *flue*, literally fluff of cotton, depicts the light hair on his arms.

2. SCOOPED FLANK: the slim waist, as if hollowed out.

2–3. LANK/ROPE-OVER THIGH: lean, with taut over-lying muscles.

3, KNEE-NAVE: knee-cap: *nave* literally = hub of a wheel.

5–6. FALL TO;/STAND AT STRESS: these are the main verbs of the one sentence so far. All the parts of Harry's body are depicted as *one crew* awaiting orders for action, *steered* by the alertness of the man's eye.

6. BARROWY: 'bulging' (from 'barrow' = mound).

7. ONEWHERE CURDED, ONEWHERE SUCKED OR SANK: the muscles (as already described) in some places are bulging or knotted (*curded*), in others tensely drawn in.

9. BEECHBOLE: trunk of a beech tree.

9–10. FINDS HIS . . . RANK/AND FEATURES IN FLESH: the main verbs of the sentence, whose subject is *each limb's barrowy brawn* (l. 6). *features in flesh* = the muscles 'manifest physically' what work they have to do.

13. QUAIL: Harry's body pliantly moves with, and yields to, the strong, uneven movement (*the wallowing*) of the plough.

14. CROSSBRIDLE: his *curls* cross and tangle in the wind.

15. WIND-LILYLOCKS-LACED: his white hair (*lilylocks*) blown into an elaborate pattern by the wind (*wind- . . . laced*). This insetting of a word between parts of a compound word is called tmesis.

16. CHURLSGRACE: the peasant's ability (Old English 'churl' = peasant).

16. CHILD OF AMANSSTRENGTH: the *churlsgrace* is the product of 'a man's strength'. The latter phrase, written as *Amansstrength*, gains a kind of strange, mythic power.

16–19. HOW IT HANGS OR HURLS/THEM etc.: *it* refers to churlsgrace; *them* refers to the *furls* or 'furrows': 'See how his peasant accomplishment suspends or hurls the furrows in a fountaining, partly glittering action, with the plough and cold furrows underneath, and with his feet racing with and along the furrows, strapped in thick, strong, wrinkled leather.'

The metre is Sprung Rhythm, with five 'official' stresses to a line, but also with extra-metrical stresses and 'hurried' and 'outriding' feet.

THAT NATURE IS A HERACLITEAN FIRE AND OF THE COMFORT OF THE RESURRECTION (July 1888) (*p. 102*)

The philosophy of Heraclitus (fl. 500 B.C.) held that all constituents of the material world were variants of the one crucial element of fire. The world was therefore characterized by the conditions of perpetual unrest, flux and movement. The sense of permanence in anything was an illusion of the senses. The true condition was one of an eternal strife between opposites, and thus never one of complete 'being' but of eternal 'becoming'. Hopkins accords with the Greek philosopher's view in seeing the tensions and opposites of a dynamically varied universe, but then turns to celebrate man's ultimately different position in the order of things, as one guaranteed immortality through Christ's resurrection.

1–2. CLOUD-PUFFBALL etc.: the first two lines describe the appearance and movement of clouds, always of particular visual interest for Hopkins.

1. CHEVY: 'scamper' or 'chase'.

3. DOWN ROUGHCAST, . . . WHITEWASH: the reference is to differently surfaced walls on which sunlight and shadows play.

4. SHIVELIGHTS: light thrown in shafted, fragmented patterns.

4. SHADOWTACKLE: shadows thrown by the elm's leaves and branches in the pattern of a ship's sail tackle.

4. LACE, LANCE, AND PAIR: verbs, suggesting the recurrent interweaving and inter-penetration of the shadows.

5. ROPES: the verb suggests the wind's own imagined shape and also its effect on things.

6. RUT PEEL: possibly the ridged, strip effects of dried mud in the ruts.

6. PARCHES: the subject of this verb is *the bright wind* (l. 5).

7. SQUANDERING OOZE: the object of *parches*. The casually-spread mud is dried by the wind, first to a kind of *dough*, then a *crust*, and then to *dust*.

7–9. STANCHES, STARCHES etc.: again, the subject of these verbs is *the bright wind* (l. 5) which 'dries out' the many layers and the footprints which *treadmire toil* has impressed (*footfretted*) in the mud.

9. NATURE'S BONFIRE: i.e. the process seen, in Heraclitean terms, as the eternal flux of growth and decay, light and shade.

Hopkins momentarily (for the next six-and-a-half lines) follows Heraclitus in seeing man, too, as simply a part of this process. But already the resistance is there to seeing man reductively and collectively as part of a process; the lines emphasize the greater tragedy when each man's unique spiritual individuality is conceived of as coming to a complete end.

10. CLEAREST-SELVÈD SPARK: man is unique because it is only in him that individuality is consciously present.

11. FIREDINT: the mark or impression made by each man's unique selfhood and identity.

12. BOTH: i.e. both the physical individual himself and his reality as impressed on others, and on the world.

14. DISSEVERAL: '*dis*tinct' and '*sever*ed'.

16. ENOUGH!: on turning from a Heraclitean train of thought, Hopkins's words (*joyless*, *dejection*) remind us obliquely that Heraclitus was known as the weeping philosopher.

20. RESIDUARY WORM: i.e. the worm which consumes what 'remains' of man.

21. AT A TRUMPET CRASH: refers to I *Corinthians* XV, 51–52 – 'we shall all be changed, in a moment, in the twinkling of an eye, at the last trump'.
23. JACK: common man.
23. POTSHERD: fragment of broken pottery.
23. PATCH: (archaic) 'a fool'.

This is a 'caudal' or 'caudated' sonnet, with three extra 'codas' of three lines each being added to the usual fourteen-line pattern (see also 'Tom's Garland', *p. 101*). The poem is in Sprung Rhythm, with many 'outriding' feet. Apart from the short ones, the lines have consistently six stresses each.

IN HONOUR OF ST. ALPHONSUS RODRIGUEZ (1888) Dublin (*p. 103*)

The subject of this tribute had been for forty years hall-porter at the College of Palma in Majorca. His description, in the sonnet's dedication, as 'Laybrother of the Society of Jesus' means that he would have accepted vows of poverty, obedience and chastity, but without being a priest. The poem was 'written to order on the occasion of the first feast since his canonization proper', and gives to a life of quiet service and inner victory the tribute usually reserved for more obvious, outward conquest.

4. FORGE: in the sense that the glory is marked visibly in the *gashed flesh* and *galled shield* of the warrior.
5. ON CHRIST THEY DO: similar strokes that *gashed* or *galled* Christ's body left on Him the stigmata, or five wounds, of the crucifixion.
6–7. BUT BE THE WAR WITHIN etc.: 'but if the war is within'; the verb 'be' governs the next two clauses as well.
8. HURTLE: the noise of violent activity.
9–10. HEWS etc.: a contrast is established between the more obvious large-scale shaping of geography and the imperceptible growth – the *trickling increment* (l. 10) – of organic things like violets and trees.
12. CONQUEST: in the form of St Alphonsus's selfless dedication and his conquest over 'evil spirits' which tormented him (according to a letter from Hopkins to Bridges).

A sonnet in standard rhythm, but with some extra-metrical stresses, and elisions.

'THOU ART INDEED JUST, LORD, IF I CONTEND' (March 1889) (*p. 104*)

Written only some three months before the poet's death. Hopkins had come to consider his five years in Ireland as 'wasted' in terms of creative results. Private retreat notes of January 1888 had contained the remark 'All my undertakings miscarry: I am like a straining eunuch'. The tone of the sonnet is a mixture of humble pleading and outraged disappointment. The Latin epigraph is from the lament of Jeremiah (*Jer*. XII, 1) and has its English equivalent in the first three lines of the poem.

7. SOTS AND THRALLS OF LUST: drunkards and slaves to lust.

9. BRAKES: thickets.

11. FRETTY CHERVIL: a wild herb with finely divided (*fretty*) parsley-like leaves.

13. WAKES: i.e. 'comes to life'.

14. MINE etc.: the force of *mine* is presumably to be dispersed throughout the line: '*My* lord, lord of *my* life, send *my* roots rain.'

The standard sonnet rhythm of the iambic pentameter should be read (Hopkins urged) '*adagio molto* and with great stress'.

'THE SHEPHERD'S BROW, FRONTING FORKED LIGHTNING, OWNS' (April 1889) (*p. 104*)

Compared to the awe-inspiring and heroic glory of God's sphere of action, man is seen as puny, awkward and trivial. The sonnet's strident cynicism made Bridges think it did not merit inclusion among the 'last serious poems'. He included it amongst the 'Fragments'. But its manuscript history shows a complete poem, seriously worked at; and its realistic appraisal of man's basic nature, when not transformed by God's grace, is one which also underlies Hopkins's other, more idealistic poems.

1. FRONTING: 'facing'.

1. OWNS: 'acknowledges'.

3. ANGELS FALL: the fate of the fallen angels connects with the *lightning* image of line 1: 'I beheld Satan as lightning fall from heaven' (*Luke*, X, 18).

7. MEMENTO MORI: used as a noun, it means 'a reminder of death': literally 'remember that you must die'.

8. VIOL: a bass-toned predecessor of the violin. cf. 'Thy pomp is brought down to the grave, and the noise of thy viols' (*Isaiah* XIV, 11). Hopkins's point, though, is that man has no profundity to merit a deep, tragic tone.

9. VOIDS: 'excretes'.

10. BLAZONED IN HOWEVER BOLD THE NAME: 'however gloriously named or renowned'.

11. MAN JACK: in Hopkins, 'Jack' denotes the ordinary, limited man. Syntax — 'The man is just Man Jack'.

11. HUSSY: 'worthless woman'.

12. DIE THESE DEATHS etc.: 'suffer the torments of this realization, and feed the *flame* of idealism'.

13. THAT . . . etc.: he breaks off, finding suddenly hopeless even the earnest piety of his own complaint against man. Instead, an image of life's vanities, further distorted like reflections in a spoon, comes to his mind.

13–14. TAME/MY TEMPESTS THERE etc.: the acceptance of life's grotesque nature 'tames' both his own idealistic strivings and his *fussy* complaints.

A sonnet in standard rhythm, but insistently counterpointed.

TO R. B. (April 1889) (*p. 105*)

The title is a dedication to Robert Bridges, and the poem an account of a feeling of creative deadlock. The sense of spiritual failure, against a background often of physical collapse, marked the final years of Hopkins's career. Here, the desolation is also claimed to affect the poet's creative powers. But it is an irony, peculiar to art in many forms, that the negative experience is expressed with an imaginative power that belies that negativity. Just as the 'terrible sonnets' achieve triumphant form while expressing trauma, the present sonnet is good poetry saying that good poetry is not possible.

1–4. THE FINE DELIGHT etc.: the flash of inspiration or feeling which, though brief in itself, prompts creative thought and plants the seed of that which will become the poem.

5–8. NINE MONTHS SHE THEN etc.: *she* = the mind, seen as pregnant with the poem (*wears*, *bears*) and finally raising and tending its offspring (*cares* and *combs*). The mind is thus the widow of the first inspiration, which 'fathered' the poem and then disappeared. But now her aim and work have been happily determined. This is the normal fruitful process which the present sonnet claims is no longer possible.

9. SWEET FIRE THE SIRE OF MUSE: i.e. the *fine delight that fathers thought* of line 1.

A sonnet in standard rhythm, but with some 'hurried' feet.

Index of Titles and First Lines